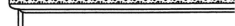

Ruth Raymond Thone

Fat—A Fate
Worse Than Death?
Women, Weight,
and Appearance

Pre-publication
REVIEW

"**R**uth Thone's *Fat—A Fate Worse Than Death?* gives us a first-class ticket for ego rehabilitation. It's a late-1990's version of ways to cope with bombardment from the media and uncaring people if you defy their approved standards. Thone is a generic therapist for everyone who marches to a different drumbeat. Her 100-item epilogue gives us a roadmap 'to fight ageism, looksism, sexism, racism, fatism.'"

Joan K. Wadlow, PhD
Chancellor,
University of Alaska-Fairbanks

Fat–A Fate
Worse Than Death?
Women, Weight, and Appearance

HAWORTH Innovations in Feminist Studies
Esther Rothblum, PhD and Ellen Cole, PhD
Senior Co-Editors

New, Recent, and Forthcoming Titles:

Fat–A Fate
Worse Than Death?
Women, Weight,
and Appearance

Ruth Raymond Thone

The Harrington Park Press
An Imprint of The Haworth Press, Inc.
New York • London

Published by The Harrington Park Press, an imprint of The Haworth Press, Inc., 10 Alice Street, Binghamton, NY 13904-1580

Selected excerpts from *Making Peace with Food* by Susan Kano. Copyright (c) 1989 by Susan Kano. Reprinted by permission of HarperCollins, Inc.

Cover design by Marylouise E. Doyle.

Library of Congress Cataloging-in-Publication Data

Thone, Ruth Raymond.
    Fat–a fate worse than death? : women, weight, and appearance / Ruth Raymond Thone.
      p. cm.
    Includes bibliographical references and index.
    ISBN 1-56023-908-5 (alk. paper)
    1. Obesity—Psychological aspects. 2. Obesity—Social aspects. 3. Overweight women. 4. Body image. I. Title.
RC552.025T48 1997
616.3'98'0019—dc21

                                      97-4041
                                        CIP

CONTENTS

ABOUT THE AUTHOR

Ruth Raymond Thone is a freelance writer, teacher, and long-time community activist in her local community and in progressive politics. The author of the books *Women and Aging: Celebrating Ourselves* (Haworth Press, 1992) and *Being Home* (1993), she is also published in several national publications. Ms. Thone is a national leader of workshops on women and aging; self-esteem; women, weight, and appearance; writing; and values realization. She is a frequent commentator on Nebraska Public Radio and is a Nebraska Humanities committee scholar/speaker.

Preface

The Beginning of a Journey

The morning newspaper headline reads: "Think Big to Camouflage Weight Gain." A story in the section devoted to what is considered soft news—entertainment, religion, art, fashion, women, housing—begins with the words "Lumpy bodies, take note." Its advice is how to take off the extra pounds put on over the holidays and "what to wear until the fat is trimmed."

I am beyond mad and am now full of rage: Is my lumpy body offensive to the obviously petite writer of this column? She looks perky—therefore petite in my eyes—in the shoulders-and-head photo that accompanies her words of wisdom. Why should I conform myself to what she and millions of others choose to look at? How do they arrive at what is pleasing and what is gross?

Trimming the fat brings images to mind of the butcher, with a very sharp knife, slicing the fat off lamb chops or steak I order for my husband's supper.

This is not the first time I've been enraged at the butchery and torture practiced on women's bodies in order for us to be what others want to look at. Nor is my morning rage unusual. It is, however, acerbated by the fact that this is January, resident month of shaping up. Weight loss, body beautification, inside house repairs, increased savings, and attempts at sobriety, are all things resolutely chosen around the New Year.

I have already withstood, beginning in January 1995, the murmurs (shouts?) of the government's War on Fat. Based on statistics that show Americans (who live in the United States) weigh more, the Surgeon General's office is preparing a national assault on fat. I have yet to hear its definition of fat or how they are going to arrange this national weight loss. Of course, it will address us in the name of health.

In a rather intense New Year's discussion at my house, my husband cloaked his displeasure with my no-longer-size-10 body and the fact that I was eating potato chips, in too-fierce insistence that he was only concerned with my high cholesterol. Later, one of his arguments went like this: "You know what your sister died of." After a moment of stunned silence, I responded, "Yes, she died of breast and lymph node cancer." His reply: "Well, her weight was part of all that."

Poor Jane. Poor me. I look in my own eyes, at four years older than the 60 at which she died, very much like my oldest sister. She had a 22-inch waist as a young woman, we used to brag, but spent her entire adult life as a large, heavy woman. My family's definition of Jane began with what she weighed or what she looked like at any moment. Her story comes later. What I am living is part of that family legacy; that is, the rule that it is not okay to weigh more than average.

After several calls to my doctor's office, in which I asked the question if breast cancer occurs more often in heavy women, I finally heard a receptionist repeat to me this message from a medical staff person: "There is a connection between obesity and cancer." The receptionist did not know the office definition of obesity. With that, I gave up the quest to have a medical answer to what I considered my husband's idiotic assertion, at least for that day.

In my "cancer" files is a lengthy *Ms.* section titled "The Politics of Cancer" (May/June 1993). Author Susan Rennie asserts, without question, that "the evidence connecting diet and breast cancer is hard to ignore." The subject is complicated, both by scientific research and by the politics of where the research money goes. "A huge body of evidence indicates," Rennie writes, "that the amount of fat a woman eats may be the link to the hormonal fluctuations implicated in breast cancer. We have known for 20 years that estrogen levels correlate with breast cancer incidence . . . where breast cancer incidence is high, estrogen levels are high, and the amount of fat eaten is high."

Without defining obesity, she continues, "Obesity, especially in postmenopausal women, also exemplifies the fat/estrogen/breast cancer linkage. Women who are overweight are at a higher risk for breast cancer because body fat itself produces estrogen, and circulating estrogens are consequently higher than in leaner women. After menopause, when natural levels of estrogen decline, excess weight becomes particularly dangerous because it keeps estrogen flowing and biologically active in breast tissue."

I doubt that my husband reads *Ms.* magazine or that he had any such research in mind.

The author Rennie automatically equates a low-fat diet with not weighing more than the average, and a high-fat diet with obesity, that is, weighing more than average, under whatever definition of obesity one operates. Over the past five years, because of high cholesterol readings, I have increased my daily exercise and considerably lowered my fat intake. Today, I am exactly the same weight, size, and shape as when I added those health regimes, and today my cholesterol is *significantly* lower. I surmise that my cholesterol went up when I quit race-walking or at least after training hard for two marathons. During the year I trained for and race-walked those two marathons, I did not lose an ounce.

My mother, who died at age 84 from various cancers beginning with breast cancer, did not have an ounce of fat on her. Her diet, probably considered healthy by ordinary standards, was undoubtedly typical of the western, high-fat diet. My husband, who has done magnificently in cutting sugar out of his diet for his type-B diabetes, eats a great deal more fat than I.

Go figure.

For a long time, I told women in my workshops that Naomi Wolf had written the definitive book on women and appearances: *The Beauty Myth: How Images of Beauty Are Used Against Women* (William Morrow & Co., Inc. 1991). I do not recommend any further work by Naomi Wolf, since I find her later work foolish and retrogressive in spirit and fact. Now I have come to recognize that the definitive book has not been written and that I can, with some authority, write out my own rage.

Despite what it might look like, I try not to blame all men for this state of affairs that keeps American women in a prison of appearance, especially that of not weighing "too much." Men are as victimized by this broad cultural edict—that women are what they look like and men are what they do—as women are. They are born into and grow up in an atmosphere of women as either caretakers or mothers or objects to be looked at, sexually and otherwise.

Women, however, are the ones who are socialized to spend a great deal of money, time, and energy on their appearances. Such issues exist for men, although in differing and lesser forms. An old friend who is a gay man expressed his irritation at my claiming certain feelings exclusive to women. He emphasized that appearance is a big issue for gay men; he is currently struggling with his weight, with special regards to how it relates to his sexual attractiveness, and also to how it affects his health and his ability to function effectively.

When I mentioned walking in the daylight-savings light of early evening "when it's still safe for a woman to be out walking," he reacted angrily, saying, "It's not safe for men to walk alone at night either." Lamely, I mentioned women's smaller size, less muscle and upper body strength, and the fact that rape is more a fact of life for women than for men. My words did little to assuage his anger, which included telling me about lesbian women choosing to be heavy and sloppy, to assert their independence from societal norms. Personal freedom from men and from patriarchal standards is what I see in lesbian women's lives, which certainly includes the permission to enjoy large, ungirdled flesh.

Women are critical of each other too. We have internalized our culture's attitudes. Women compete for men, for jobs, for grants, for attention, for pensions—and wind up considering other women "the problem" or "the enemy." That's easy enough for me to understand, having spent a lifetime saying and hearing women say "She sure has gained weight . . . let herself go . . . was so beautiful when she was young . . . looks terrible in that outfit . . . has gotten old and heavy" (as if it were wrong to do so).

Spending so much energy and time on this subject may seem trivial compared to war, famine, and increasing violence in our society. Yet women's imprisonment, socialized as we are to think that we have to be a certain weight or look a certain way, keeps us floundering in low self-esteem, our contributions to the larger issues of life languishing for want of time, energy, and confidence.

Right now, we are experiencing the *backlash* that is brilliantly and thoroughly described by Susan Faludi in *Backlash: The Undeclared War Against American Women* (Crown Publishers, 1991).

Women are to be smaller, less assertive, feminine equated with one's size and behavior, careful of men's egos, ever-nurturing to children, taking up less space physically and psychically, all the while denying that we are being judgmental of ourselves or others.

As long as we don't talk about this subject, or trivialize it, we can pretend it doesn't exist. But you'd have to be living like a hermit, far away and with no contact with *any* commerce—newspapers, TV, billboards, stores, doctors, computers, all the millions of daily interactions we have between and among ourselves—in order not to have some comprehension of the magnitude of this issue for women. Women say they *choose* to go on diets, lose weight, or dress fashionably, without reckoning the power over themselves, the seductive impact of constantly being told "You look wonderful, did you just lose weight?" and having their appearance be the instant and never-ending subject.

I call myself old and heavy, not to be self-critical, but to live in reality. By that, I do not mean that I am tired, crabby, inactive, dispirited, or *not attractive*. It is simply a way of declaring the truth, no matter how we like to pretty things up with euphemisms, denial, and exhortations to be positive and "up."

A young woman, commenting on this work, writes, "Do you really want your reader to portray you as [old and heavy]? I can't help thinking that in order to put such emphasis on looks in the first place you must be highly insecure with yourself. I do not mean to offend you, but it startles me a little. . . . If being thin helps one's self-esteem, wouldn't you encourage their efforts?" Her reaction to the $33 billion spent annually in the United States on weight-loss products and services is to lament, "That is devastatingly ridiculous. If a person inside wants to be thin, then regular exercise and watching what one eats is enough." Ah, the innocence of youth, *and* the carefully-nourished-by-extraordinary-media-effort idea that we can easily control our size and weight and that if our "soul" is beautiful and *our body thin*, so are we.

I read and loan out and copy chapters from several really fine books, magazines, and radical essays about women and eating, women and body size, women and beauty, women and appearances. The increase of these is evidence of a backlash beginning against *the* backlash and of some strong efforts—books, TV shows, magazine articles, discussions on the internet, 'zines (small, personally published, often radical magazine-style publications, usually dedicated to a specific subject and not commercially distributed)—to save young women from anorexia and bulimia, and to save other women from all the vicious stereotyping of the "obese" and "overweight" and, occasionally, from the appearance police.

One has to be very careful about which books, magazines, and programs to buy, literally and figuratively. Many current programs that advertise "health" are simply weight-loss programs in disguise, wolves in sheeps' clothing. A parallel example is that of companies that produce alcohol products trumpeting their programs about safe driving and advertising that they are against teenage and heavy drinking. Obviously, that is the fox in the chicken coop. Many alcohol and drug-abuse programs accept money from the alcohol industry. Getting young people started on alcohol use is of great importance to these industries, as are the majority of profits to be made from heavy to abusive drinkers. A new report from the Marin Institute for the Prevention of Alcohol and Other Drug Problems (in *Backgrounder*, September 1996) gives statistics from a research team led by Thomas Greenfield, senior scientist at the Alcohol Research Group in Berkeley, California. This research demonstrates that "drinking in hazardous amounts [5 or more drinks a day] accounts for more than 53 percent of all drinking reported by U.S. drinkers." "At risk" drinking, which is, according to the latest federal alcohol guidelines, three to four drinks a day, accounts for 25 percent of all drinking, and "moderate drinking," one to two drinks a day, accounts for only 22 percent of all drinking. "The top 5 percent of drinkers . . . account for more than 40 percent of all alcohol drunk in the United States." "The alcohol industry claims it wants its products drunk in moderation," yet, Greenfield says, "these findings highlight the fact that its market depends considerably on heavy and binge drinking, mostly by young men."

It comes up over and over again in me, not only the rage, but the terrible need to speak out, to scream, to document, to reflect on, to write as much as I can, about my journey through this thicket of culturally imposed self-hate. Healing comes for me through writing. When I write my way through something, the stories leave me at a different place than when I started.

Artist Willem deKooning says to me from one of the several clippings taped above my workplace, "The attitude that nature is chaotic and that the artist puts order into it is a very absurd point of view, I think. All that we can hope for is to put some order into ourselves." May Sarton, in *At Seventy*, reflected that image when she wrote, "I have never written a book that was not born out of a question I needed to answer for myself . . . art is order but it is made out of the chaos of life."

I write during crisis, as I did for the months during which Jane, my oldest sister, was dying; I have an unpublished manuscript written throughout the last months of a painful political campaign in 1982; I wrote my way through my mother's death in 1991, from the moment of the call from my sister Ann telling me that our mother had less than two months to live. Some people clean the garage, needlepoint like fury, plant gardens, drink too much, watch TV all the time, or stay busy in some other way to get through things. Even without crisis, I write stories in my head about life, only from that singular vantage point that is mine, and then write them down on paper. It is, for me, a way of finding my way through, of figuring out, understanding, facing the truth of, and coming to terms with this rich, bewildering existence.

In this work of accepting myself as a heavy woman, an old woman, in the midst of deep, cultural prejudices, the only way out is through. I constantly try to see my body as thinner than it is, and in some secret corner of my mind keep the dim hope that I will be thin again, or better yet, that I will someday come to see myself as beautiful—pounds, lumps, gray hair, unfashionable clothing, and all. None of this "in the eye of the beholder stuff." As Cynthia Rich writes so powerfully, the idea is not to see beyond the wrinkles or the skin of different color, but to see those wrinkles and that skin color themselves as beautiful, worthy of our respect, attention, and admiration.

"It's all downhill from here" is a frequent jest about the last third of life, that time whenever we begin to think of aging and know more deeply that there is an end to our life and we're getting closer to it. *This* journey is actually uphill, an Outward Bound trip through the wilderness of living in a place where value is determined by what someone thinks you look like, and where the joking adage that "you can't be too rich or too thin" wreaks havoc on most American women.

Thinking to write an epilogue to these chapters, I wrote off the top of my head, as it were, a long, questioning essay, trying to corral all my end-of-the-book doubts. Since it asks more questions than it answers, and demonstrates, as more than one woman in a writing class said, enormous personal insecurity, I decided to make it Chapter 2. That *is* how I feel sometimes. Surely I must not, at nearly 65, live out my mother's adage never to write a letter when you're "down." Any reluctance to be vulnerable, to express my doubts and my rage, plays into the old upbringing that insists we only present happy faces to the world and to one another. Another *beauty myth*.

I am heartened by Susan Tiberghien's words in *Looking for Gold*, the record of her brave journey through dream analysis: "How many of us conceal, consciously or unconsciously, our pain, our suffering, our despair? How many of us write about the joy of childbirth without writing about its agony?" She quotes Carolyn Heilbrun in *Writing a Woman's Life* (Ballantine Books, NY, 1988): "There will be narratives of female lives only when women no longer live their lives isolated in the houses and stories of men." Heilbrun looks forward to when women, "born into the women's movement and escaping the usual rhythms of the traditional female existence, discover the freedom and courage to take risks, to be courageous, to write their own story."

Tiberghien also reminds me of May Sarton's words in that first, most wonderful journal, *Journal of a Solitude* (Norton, 1977), in which Sarton passionately and courageously writes, "At some point I believe one has to stop holding back for fear of alienating some imaginary reader or real relative or friend, and come out with personal truth."

It is past time, at least for me, to grow beyond those old boundaries between the personal and the political, and beyond those old family rules against telling family tales outside of the family, the rules that say "Don't feel, don't talk." I choose to live in a world where I can express all I feel, including what, in this land of cheerful extraversion, we call negative emotions and thoughts. This writing, this work, is for me the sure way to the joy of living a life congruent with my insides, consistent with my hard-won values, and toward growing into wholeness.

SECTION I:
MY OWN TRUTHS

Chapter 1

Welcome to the World Beyond Size 10

What is the worst thing someone ever said to you about your appearance or size?

Even as that question brought forth awful, hard-to-believe stories, it eventually sent my friends and I into gales of laughter, tears streaming down our cheeks as we relieved for ourselves the terrible tension under which many large women live in this culture.

My leading candidate for the person who said the worst thing to me used to be the time I went to a particular AA meeting I'd not gone to for several months, where an old friend always celebrated his sobriety anniversary. After the meeting, that old friend greeted me by patting my stomach and saying "On the nest again, are we?" The suggestion of pregnancy to this 60-year-old woman was his way of pretending to be funny in commenting on my increased weight.

I thought I'd die, and said some "funny," stupid thing to him to cover up. Of course I didn't say, "What gives you the right to comment on my size? Do I comment on what you look like? Are you at all interested in who I am or just in what you think I am supposed to look like? Do you know how much that remark hurts me?"

However, one summer, that friend's "jest" took second place when another acquaintance won first place in the dreadful remark contest. Again, at an AA meeting where I went to mark my sixteenth sobriety anniversary, a man who had not seen me in years said, after the meeting, "When you came in, I poked Bob and said, 'I haven't seen her in 40 pounds. Ha. Ha. Ha.'" He laughed hard at his great joke. I laughed, too, to cover up the fact that I'd just taken a direct hit to the body, called him a jackass, and then changed the subject.

I did not say, "Thanks for the anniversary present. I see you haven't changed and still think junior high behavior is funny, that you haven't budged out of the adolescence we all come into recovery from. Did you think I wanted to hear that? Do you consider that your own personal honesty? Are you glad to see me or have you been trained over a lifetime to consider fat ugly and to see only thin women as worthy of respect?"

A festering resentment began upon hearing that a friend commented to another that I had gained 100 pounds since she saw me last and was shocked. I wanted to scream "I haven't gained that much!" Another friend asked why I did not direct my anger at the "friend" who repeated the hurtful remark back to me.

The late Stephen Butterfield wrote in "On Being Unable to Breathe" in *The Sun* (March 1988, pp. 10-16) about an illness he struggled with, "Superfluity must go . . . What is superfluous? Anger that freezes into resentment; jealousy; greed; gossip; ego-clinging; pretense; embarrassment; any form of fixation; running after pleasure; the discursive thought that maintains the story-line of *me*. These things are very costly, in terms of the life-energy that it takes to keep them going."

Jungian analyst Aldo Carotenuto, professor in theory of personality at the University of Rome, writes, ". . . . What is essential is the resolution of inner conflicts, which are what give others the possibility of injuring us, and above all take away our ability to express our true individuality (*The Vertical Labyrinth: Individuation in Jungian Psychology*, Inner City Books, 1985, p. 13).

Last summer, I greeted an old friend by commenting on how thin he is. I knew from his wife that he has attended Overeaters Anonymous for years and that his attention to food issues has produced *some* good in their life together. Later I realized that I complimented him quickly about his thinner size in order to forestall his possible commenting on my increased weight. By jumping immediately into his value of thinness, maybe I could keep him from saying something awful to me. It worked and I felt uncomfortable about it.

I remember reluctantly that time in O'Hare airport, when my husband, a Congressional colleague of his, and I were between planes. The friend, in what may have been a compliment on my appearance said, "You love it, don't you, knowing that people think you're good-looking, that people (read: men) are looking at you." I was stunned. I not only did not consider myself attractive, but at that time was oblivious of other people's attention, positive or otherwise. It is not surprising that I remember exactly what I looked like then: I was a size 10, wore a bright-red knit dress and high heels, had soft-brown-dyed hair, and wore makeup. I can still hear the anger in his remarks, even though we considered ourselves good friends.

Now I say to my grown daughters, all of whom criticize their bodies, want to weigh less, and think they are fat, "Appreciate it while you are this size," not even what could be considered slightly over the average weight. I wish I had.

I never knew how much I unconsciously depended on "looking good," until I grew out my hair to its natural gray-silver and quit having it "done," blow-drying it after showers and swimming. Later, I decided I had injured my body enough with my last diet, began to wear only comfortable clothing and footwear, especially Birkenstocks, and wore less makeup, if any. As Erica Jong says in *Fear of Fifty*, "The beauty trap is deeper than you thought" (Preface, p. xviii).

I never was very good at makeup, buying my first eye shadow in my thirties at a theatrical makeup store in New Orleans' French Quarter with an equally late-blooming friend; my daughters used to say I looked like a raccoon when they were not telling me to rub in my blush.

There are degrees of becoming old and large. My sense of it is that since 1984 I have gained weight, over the years gradually becoming what is now called heavy (although mostly we say "too heavy"). My current weight, which I guess at since I haven't weighed myself for years, and size, have been stable for about three years. Sometimes I am okay with that and sometimes not. I am intentional about and hope to become comfortable with myself, my clothing, my appearance.

A funny thing happened to me on the way to keynote a conference on aging one year. The *Omaha World-Herald*, which is the dominant Nebraska newspaper, used my picture in the spring of 1993 to illustrate a conference on women and aging at which I was speaking. Several men mentioned seeing the picture and story to me, their comments along the line of asking, without actually saying, "You sure looked good in that picture. How old is it?" Not a single woman spoke in that vein, although they commented "That's a good picture" and congratulated me on speaking at the conference. I felt, as I wrote to a friend, as if I'd done something wrong. I checked my files and found that the picture had been taken three years before. What I had done wrong was to age and to go around not "fixed up" all the time with dress-up clothes, makeup, and hair "done." A very telling experience on the way to a conference on aging!

The rules for women are very severe. Years ago, my husband and I lamented the appearance of a woman's fat, drooping upper arms. She had been very beautiful, we said to one another, and agreed that now that she was obviously getting old, she shouldn't wear things that let her upper arms show. Now I demand of him, when he comments that a certain woman is "attractive," to tell me if that means thin and young-looking, with dyed hair, stylish clothes, and fashionable shoes. He protests that he does not notice!

The list of things women are not to do is led by DO NOT GET FAT, which has become an obsession that has led millions of young women to develop eating disorders and even grade school youngsters to diet and comment compulsively about their size.

We are always to keep our legs together, or sit cross-legged or with our ankles crossed. Not only does leg-crossing destroy tissue and veins, but it is difficult for large women to observe this cultural edict.

We are to choose our clothing for how "slimming" it is—no horizontal stripes, no baggy shapes, dark and solid colors if one is heavy. Clothing for large women is exploding some of these old strictures. With the average American woman having a height of 5'3" and weighing 144 pounds, makers of women's clothing are finally designing garments for the not-thin and not-tiny market.

We are to consider ourselves "bad" and "naughty" if we eat with abandon or if we forget our current weight-loss program. We fear the upcoming holidays, our own sugar binges, and keep secret what we eat in the kitchen as we fix another's food. At parties, we don't heap our plates with food in order to maintain the fiction that dainty women don't eat a lot.

Women are to dress to please men—wear high heels that make buttocks sway, pinch in waists to emphasize slimness, lift up bosoms to call attention to the size and firmness of breasts, cover up body parts that are not considered attractive, look attractive but not too attractive, shave legs and armpits, paint faces and finger and toe nails, and smell "good," taking special care to cover up any body smells.

We are to exercise a lot to keep our shape and "tone"; lie in the sun or under tanning machines to keep our skin just the right, fashionable shade of brown; and keep our self-esteem up and a man interested by having eye tucks, face-lifts, liposuction on our thighs and stomachs—all of which are euphemisms for having our bodies and faces cut up, at great financial, emotional, and physical cost to ourselves.

Every visit to the doctor's office will require us to be weighed, even if we are there to get a prescription for a stubborn cold. Nurses and medical assistants are usually personally affronted at my insistence that I not be weighed. How dare I disobey the system, a system only concerned with my health at that! We are constantly reminded that almost every disease or complaint could be fixed if we just lose weight.

In a women's history class, I once heard a woman who has worked years in medical records reporting that 99.99 percent of the charts she looks at and files begin with "obese, white, female." That is an amazing statistic. Another young woman found Slim-Fast in the refrigerator of her 80-year-old, 100-pound grandmother. "Oh, look at these fat cheeks," her grandmother explained to justify the diet liquid. Another young woman's 79-year-old, 120-pound grandmother told her, "My doctor wants me to lose more weight."

I am continually amazed and further horrified at these common, constant stories of abuse against women, and of the medical professions' stance that whatever ails us will be fixed by losing weight.

Helen Luke, old woman and Jungian analyst, tells of the ultimate aging journey that gives to our enemies as well as to those we love "the freedom to be themselves." This final struggle surely includes ourselves, and is argued against by hundreds of images that swarm around and soak into our consciousness each and every day.

Since I have become heavier, I get to learn what large women have always known: that people have no compunctions against talking negatively about large people, especially women, even in front of them. Somehow they think they have an inalienable right to judge and comment on fat people, especially women. I am sorry that I didn't know earlier in my life how the rest of the world treats large women.

We all arrive at this strange time of becoming someone we've never been before by different paths. My friend Linda Hellerich Tuttle has struggled since early childhood against weighing "too much," beginning with diet pills, provided by a doctor to whom her mother took her, when she was eight years old. I have been a size 8 or 10 for most of my adult life, although never unaware for a single minute of the dreadful possibility of becoming chubby. Weight and the control of it was an ordinary and constant subject in my house growing up. We were perfect reflections in the cultural mirror.

I am constantly dismayed at how difficult it is to live in this culture as a fat woman while at the same time hanging onto a healthy sense of one's values and worth.

I was confused and angry at a discussion in my *own* living room one time when my Spanish class gathered for a social occasion. We were saying good-bye to Connie who was returning to Chile with her husband and new baby after several years in the United States. For some odd reason, the women were talking about the "cause" of women becoming fat, probably projecting their own fears of it onto other women. Connie, who was a psychology graduate student, was explaining that she had discovered that women who have a hard time separating from their mothers become fat. Lamely and unsuccessfully, I tried to discount this theory, all the time wanting to scream, "Don't any of you realize you are sitting here passing judgment on me? How dare you act as if I don't exist during your pretentious discussion of fat women! What makes you think there's something 'wrong' with large women?" But I didn't do anything except to feel bad and bewildered when they left.

Genes, metabolism, and lifestyle determine weight and body size. I know that. Yet I am still caught in cultural edicts that say fat people eat too much, fat people are lazy, fat people are out of control, fat people have let themselves go, fat people should "do something about their weight," fat people are unhealthy, and fat people are not attractive. None of the above is true, and all are negative judgments about what another looks like.

Freeing ourselves from the diet-weight obsession is a long process of unlearning and continuing to object to and expose the fallacies and idiocies of our cultural conditioning.

Instead of reveling in a friend's first baby years ago, another college friend and I ate the delicious lunch the new mother had prepared, peeked at the baby put away in another room, and marveled out loud at how the friend had gotten her figure back so fast. She protested that she was still too fat. Could anyone have told us that at that moment we were participating in genocide against women, in an insanity with which we had been infected? If they had, we would have disagreed with and certainly disparaged them. We knew better. We knew how wonderful we were, young, bright, and minions of the culture to our last breath.

Well, not quite the last breath, thank god. Renowned therapist Karen Horney says that life is a very effective therapist, although a cruel one. I am certainly learning a lot about being a large, old woman in a culture that values, most highly, thinness and youth. What this extraordinary journey into old age and self-acceptance teaches me is the depth of my own arrogance, the breadth of my ignorance, the tenacity of my lifelong desire for external affirmation. Most especially and joyfully, I am experiencing my own decision-making powers and abiding ability to change and be responsible for my life.

Chapter 2

Doubt: Whistling in the Dark

What sort of head-in-the-sand trick am I up to? Am I denying the reality of actual standards of beautiful and ugly, the reality that women are considered ornaments?

How many meanings of beauty do we subscribe to? Must I rail against the "political and economic uses of its standardization"? (Ninotchka Rosca in a review of *Beauty Queens on the Global Stage: Gender, Contests, and Power*, by Cohen, Wilk, and Stoeltje, Routledge, 1996.) In my heart I know I am not Don Quixote tilting at windmills, but sometimes, in the down and critical times, I am tempted to think so.

Not only do I keep having arguments with my daughters on the subject of this entire book and my anger about appearance requirements for women in this country, but I find myself embarrassed to tell someone the subject of my latest efforts, thinking the subject to be trivial in the face of the world's horrors and absurdities.

"The girls," all now in their thirties, and I have long had discussions about the wisdom, the appropriateness, the value, and the necessity of painting faces, wearing jewelry, fixing one's hair, adorning one's body with clothing. They are apprehensive, I think, that their mother, now old and heavy, may be throwing the baby out with the bathwater, in her anger at appearance standards for women, which fall most heavily on the old and the fat.

I am lucky beyond words that my three grown daughters and I are good friends, the good surfacing after some difficult years when they were growing up—their parents full-time in politics, their mother an active alcoholic, and their family painfully stuck in that family disease and other dysfunctions.

To the youngest daughter Amy, I rail against thin women following the establishment rules of acceptance. She insists that not all thin women are victims of this cultural edict. "But they all can pass and not relinquish their establishment credentials," I insist to her, trying somehow to stake out some ground of legitimacy for how I feel.

Marie insists that her boyfriend's delight in her appearance is based simply on the fact that men are more visual and that survival genes require them to support their partners, neither of which I find believable. She also mentions the need to procreate, appropriate at her age, but hardly an excuse for 60-year-old men wanting women half their age or less on their aging arms, although we are treated these days to stories of second families, accompanied by emphasis on these second chances to be a wonderful father.

Anna and I have been so busy arranging a second trip to Palestine/Israel these days that we have not settled into any familiar discussions about women's size, weight, hair, or clothing. Actually, since she has had two back surgeries in the past year, perhaps she cannot afford to give her energy to such comparatively ephemeral concerns, ones that cause less acute pain than a badly herniated disk, chronic pain a different matter.

Talking with my friend on the telephone, I cringe when she wants to know what I am eating as we talk, and upon hearing low-fat cottage cheese and reduced-fat potato chips, calls my lunch "junk food." Later, she admitted she was just mad that she could not eat either of those foods, allergic as she is to a great many foods.

I threw up my hands as an old friend I'd not seen in years and I ate lunch and had one more talk about my work on appearance issues for women. "When did you start to gain weight?"; "When did you stop dieting?"; and "When did you begin to feel like this . . . turn your attention to this?" she asked. I felt interrogated and defensive, as if I'd done something wrong by becoming fat and insisting that I was old. She insisted she was unaware of the prejudice against large/fat women in our culture. I am reminded of that woman counselor with whom I worked while I was in treatment for alcoholism, who asked me, "When did you start to wear blue jeans?" and told me I had, unconsciously or not, begun then to try to destroy my husband's political career by dressing in a manner that was then considered indicative of youthful rebellion and the middle class.

Do I need to "get over it", and sooner than later? Is this abuse of women not a substantive issue in the world we live in today? As

I've asked before, am I simply angry that I am old and heavy, no longer one of the elect? Did I give up playing the game and yet still want to be a player?

If I ignore it, will it go away? Can I choose and *decide* to dress and do my hair in a way that makes the best of my current size, age, and appearance? That would require hiring someone to tell me what to do, what to buy, how to cut my hair—and all with the idea of making me "attractive" beyond my normal looks. Do I want to give in to the appearance police and women's jailers to accomplish that?

Do I want to continue to be affronted at each day's countless indignities and be obsessed with the subject of age and weight? Is my skin litmus paper, turning a bilious green at any insult, my body a Geiger counter, going into clicking spasms as I approach the insulting person or institution? How do I fight back, without demeaning myself, without encouraging others' stereotypes and prejudices, while finding comfort and growth? Some days I think to give it all up. Yet how does one give up caring about something one cares deeply about?

I can find courage and support from what I know is a deeper reality, which Ade Bethune speaks to: "To seek after beauty as an end is a wild goose chase, a will-o'-the-wisp, because it is to misunderstand the very nature of beauty, which is *the normal condition of a thing being as it should be*" (*The Sun*, June 1996, p. 40).

The same article quotes Miguel de Unamuno: "Cure yourself of the affliction of caring how you appear to others. Concern yourself only with how you appear before God, concern yourself only with the idea God may have of you." Even without GOD in my life, I understand. Concern yourself with your inner wisdom, with your creativity, with your truthfulness, with that deep center that knows better than to accept external approval or disapproval as the guiding standard of your life.

Is a disillusioned partner's "parting salvo—'I no longer find you attractive'" (Jennifer Yeo in *The Sun*, June 1996) to be taken seriously, sending us into deep gloom or chasing after an ephemeral face or body that will hold another's love?

Is insisting we get over the inequality among women, which is determined by arbitrary, random standards of beauty, akin to that old liberal shibboleth that we are to become color-blind? Color-blind no longer works for me, if it ever did, suggesting as it does that we not do the harder work of truly accepting *all* that another is, including one's skin color. All colors, sizes, shapes, sexes, ethnic backgrounds, ages, and classes must become simply part of the rich fabric of who we are, living together on one small planet.

Writing "On Being Beautiful" in the June 1996 *The Sun*, Nancy Huston, holding the opinion that we are rather foolish to ignore bodies and their effects on all our interactions, insists,

> "People who study well and write good papers, whether they are beautiful or ugly, brown or yellow, tall or short, should receive good grades; and people who have appropriate qualifications and experience should never need to consent to being sodomized by the powers that be in order to get a job or a degree or a promotion. The role of beauty—and every other culturally or genetically inherited factor—in such situations as legal trials, political elections, thesis defenses, and tenure hearings should be as close to zero as possible. In public life . . . modern democratic institutions are rightly required to be blind to physical traits. At the opposite end of the spectrum lies lovemaking . . . in between the two there is social existence. . . . This crucial middle ground is currently being eroded to nothingness in the US by maniacal moralism and ludicrous legalism. . . ." (pp. 26-29)

Are all my "we should," "we must," and "we ought" akin to Prohibitionist Carrie Nation axing taverns, attacking the symptom, not the roots? Throwing feathers into a storm? Shouting against the wind?

Huston's ultimate point is that "all of us play the game according to the cards we have in our hand. . . one deals with what is dealt" and confesses that her "daughter is also turning out to be beautiful and intelligent, which means that, in addition to teaching her to eschew boasting about it, I shall need to teach her certain things about what sort of treatment she can expect at the hands of the world. . . . "

That is certainly *one* way of approaching this whole subject, indeed one based on the existence of an absolute standard of beauty—and quite as surely, ugliness.

In an industry in which London *Guardian* interviewer Beverley D'Silva observes that "obesity remains a hangable offence," actress

Sally Field claims her "bad old body image was not just a side-effect of the industry's demands, but is "typical of every woman in the United States who watches TV and reads magazines, and ends up thinking: If this is what beautiful is, I'm not it." Admitting she is "still possessed," Field "went running for an hour this morning. One part of me knows it's the best cure for jet lag, the other just wants to stay thin."

We live and move and have our being in that ambivalence, exercising because we know it's good for us, and secretly hoping we stay thin or become thin in the bargain, one aspect of the Faustian bargain women live under these days.

Reviewer Judy Hunt describes current evidence of this ambivalence in *The New York Times*, writing about feminist Letty Cottin Pogrebin's new book *Getting Over Getting Older* (Little, Brown & Co., 1996): "Others may be confused by what seem like contradictions, such as Pogrebin scolding women who spend hours hiding signs of age, while she tries to enhance her own appearance ('her long streaked blond hair is artificially colored . . .' and 'I wear lipstick and perfume around the house, even when there's no one around . . .')"

In a new health and fitness column in the *Omaha World-Herald*, a recent collection of information warns about the side effects of olestra, that "fat-free fat," which causes abdominal cramping and fat-soluble vitamins and carotenoids to wash out of the body, perhaps during the diarrhea it also causes.

I read on to "another reason not to yo-yo diet." Linking losing and regaining weight to poor self-esteem and depression, director of the Behavioral Medicine Research Center at Baylor College of Medicine, Dr. John Foreyt, remarks that "successful weight maintainers had a greater sense of well-being, a lower stress level and better *control* of their eating."

It's subtle but very devastating: *You* are responsible for yo-yo dieting, *not* diets; *not* prejudice against you for your size; *not* a culture that makes thin the only socially appropriate size; *not* doctors who recommend losing weight for nearly everything; *not* insurance companies that list ridiculously low weights as average and supposedly possible for everyone; *not* stores and catalogs whose dress sizes only go to 14; *not* the media and Hollywood, which represent fat people as only jolly or dysfunctional; *not* women socialized to find their value in what someone else thinks of their appearance; *not* purveyors of exercise programs, exercise machines, and eating regimes; *not* people who voice the most outrageous prejudices and criticisms of heavy women.

Am I obsessed? Does my anger trigger the "enemy?" Must I go deeply into eastern wisdom literature, learning Akido as a way of facing the world, listening carefully to the *I Ching* that counsels one not to provoke opposition by my offense against the world I live in? Do I provide the target by constantly being aware of what the culture tells me I must do to be valued? Would ignoring it make it go away or at least make it easier to live with?

This week, I ordered four new books. These current works evidence that we as a society are being made more aware of the dysfunction, the pain, and the ludicrousness of narrow, unrealistic, tortuous appearance standards, especially for women: *Am I Thin Enough Yet? The Cult of Thinness and the Commercialization of Identity* (Sharlene Hesse-Biber, Oxford University Press, 1996), *Look at My Ugly Face: Myths and Musings on Beauty and Other Perilous Obsessions with Women's Appearance* (Sara Halprin, Penguin Books, 1995), *The Invisible Woman: Confronting Weight Prejudice in America* (W. Charisse Goodman, Gurze Books, 1995), and *Love the Body You Were Born With* (Monica Dixon, Berkley Publishing Group, 1996). I found all four of these books to be excellent, especially Goodman's, then proceeded to check out from the library three more: Cheri Erdman's *Nothing to Lose, a Guide to Sane Living in a Larger Body* (HarperCollins, 1995), *Love Your Looks: How to Stop Criticizing and Start Appreciating Your Appearance* by Carolynn Hillmann (Fireside Books, Simon and Schuster, 1995), and *Self-Esteem Comes in All Sizes* by Carol A. Johnson (Doubleday, 1996).

In addition to these and other well-researched and courageous writings, do I need to *stop* reading advertisements that ask "Do You **HATE** Your Weight?" or doctors' columns headlined "The biochemistry of obesity" (in the health column of the *Lincoln Journal Star*, March 3, 1996), although one Dr. Peter Gott writes, " . . . a majority of obese persons cannot shed pounds, even if they reduce caloric consumption to an unhealthful, ridiculously tiny amount. . . .

The balance [between fat deposition and caloric intake] is upset in obesity." That same doctor's column reports (in the June 6, 1996, *Lincoln Journal Star*), "In the past, gallbladder attacks were pretty much confined to the 4 F's: fat, female, fair, and over forty." I qualify, having had my gall bladder removed a year ago—my doctor says gall bladder disease comes from Western eating habits. Something in me resents the 4-F category, that old shorthand description of someone who is unfit to serve (originally in World War II). Do I flail against semantics? Do I need a better sense of humor?

Another news story, carried in the May 30, 1996, *Omaha World-Herald*, reports that weight-loss centers withhold "their programs' cost, length, effectiveness and safety as well as the qualifications of the staff. . . . Last year, 7.5 million people spent more than $1.7 billion at commercial weight-loss centers. The five largest are Jenny Craig, Nutri/Systems, Diet Center, Physicians Weight Loss Centers, and Weight Watchers International. Some 48 million people—one-fourth of the U.S. population—are currently dieting, spending more than $33 billion annually on weight-loss products and services."

Utahan Lynn Romer has designed the "Pinocchio Plot" as part of her personal crusade against looksism, which she defines as the judging of character by physical appearance. She suggests alternatives for both children's and adult's reading, and wants to change the world, reports a recent wire service story in the June 9, 1996, *Lincoln Journal-Star*, by AP writer David Foster. She is quoted to say, "I'm ugly. What's wrong with that?" she asks. "I'm ugly and please don't try to tell me I'm not because if you do then I'm going to think there's something wrong with being ugly. It's OK to be ugly. I think I have a beautiful soul, and that's all that matters."

A newspaper photograph accompanying the Associated Press story about Romer, the childhood in which she was called ugly, and the desertion by a fiancée who "couldn't fall in love with an ugly woman," is not a woman ugly by any standards. If she thinks her nose is too big, and the stupid guy dumped her because of her looks, I think they're both wrong, socialized by this insidious insistence on a certain appearance for women. A pleasantly attractive, positive, apparently confident woman is what I see in Lynn Romer's picture. But she's fighting the right enemy, I'd say—a culture that calls her ugly and therefore lesser than so-called beautiful women; a patriarchy that judges women on some subjective, tiny, random scale of attractiveness; and her own internalized low self-esteem from being born female and judged for years.

The *Fat!So?* 'zine recently ran a readers' survey asking, "What do you like about being fat?" The answers reprinted in *UTNE Reader* (May-June 1996) were fun and wonderful, powerful and superbly creative. My first issue of *Fat!So?* I read immediately from cover to cover, loving its irreverence and its factual, funny, and affirming contents.

Coco Chanel, of clothing and perfume fame and skinny as a rail, as I remember photographs of her in magazines and newspapers, said "Adornment is never anything except a reflection of the heart" (quoted in Ann Wilson Schaef's *Meditations for Women Who Do Too Much*, Harp, 1990, entry for June 11). That remark reminds me of what I call the "bathrobe" story. In discussing broadening appearance standards for women, especially old women, an acquaintance who directs a senior center told me how the women began dressing better, wearing makeup, and combing their hair, as they increased their self-esteem by attending the programs at the center, "getting out of their bathrobes," as she said. She considered this evidence of their coming out of age- and solitude-caused depression. I cannot refute her story; yet I caution women in my classes to be careful not to judge people by their clothing, neatness, hair, cosmetics, or by a single standard set by the culture we live in—a culture heavily influenced by northern European immigration a century ago, this leftover Puritan culture, this land dominated by consumerism. Surely there are wild, wonderful, brilliant women in this world, who are rightly depressed because they do not pass the appearance standards we have in this country, ones which we use as evidence of mental health.

I recently stumbled across a birthday card that had the text "Happy Birthday to a good friend who's been with me through thick and thin" written over a photo of two heavy, grinning, unfashionably dressed women, and that finished with "and chunky and plumpy and chubby and porky." Nice words, right, to describe us? I don't know how I feel about that card, except embarrassed and down. Old Lesbians Organized for Change (OLOC), a superb activist organization headquartered in Houston, Texas (PO Box 980422,

Houston, TX 77098), has a well-organized campaign against sexist, racist, and ageist birthday cards. OLOC also speaks against injustice against old lesbian women, even in lesbian groups, organizes conferences, publishes a professional newsletter, joins boycotts, and monitors all media for blatant and subtle prejudice.

A 12-step program that has saved my life from alcoholism describes those of us who qualify for its healing parameters as on occasion acting like the baby as king, demanding of those around him or her attention and obedience to its wants. I do fit that description at times, though surely not now. Despite the male, Christian emphasis of the literature of Alcoholics Anonymous, and the license that provides those who are comfortable within and supportive of those patriarchal parameters, I find the comraderie and acceptance in AA meetings to be enormously helpful. I am strongly drawn to the work of Charlotte Kasl, psychologist, recognized expert on addiction, social activist, and author of *Women, Sex, and Addiction* (Ticknor and Fields, 1989, and Harper Perennial, 1990) and *Finding Joy* (HarperCollins, 1994). Her 16 steps address ways women can heal and become whole in this culture.

What is more an issue of justice than accepting women of all sizes, shapes, appearances, and treating them fairly and thoughtfully, especially to those of us working to destroy this women's prison of appearance? I think negatively and critically of myself during times of being too tired, my life too full of extraversion, not enough sleep, nor enough quiet, alone, and unscheduled time.

The lovely movie by Dutch filmmaker Marleen Gorris, *Antonia's Line*, has majestic Dutch actress Willeke Van Ammelrooy as Antonia say, in great good wisdom and wry humor, "Life just has to be lived, that's all"—this said in the midst of births, deaths, suicides, love affairs, accidents, and other vagaries of their family's generations. Yes, and lived as it is given to us, or presents itself to us, as we follow the call on our hearts.

This cause, this work, is mine, despite all arguments and attitudes to the contrary. It is one I care deeply about, and over which I am willing to expose my rage and desire, adding my weight to the eventual triumph of the collaborative life, one in which we do not, in any way, do each other in, even in setting requirements for what others must look like in mine or another's eyes.

Chapter 3

For You, Jane, Too Late?

Years ago, I designed a four-week class on "FAT: Women, Weight, and Appearance." Four women signed up, all size 14 and under, who thought they were fat. One woman came fresh from an office contest where one department was pitted against another to lose weight.

We had a wonderful, difficult time. Little did I know that this was not the beginning of a sought-after new teaching. Later, my friend Linda and I designed and led workshops titled "Women, Weight, and Appearance." People did not exactly line up for our classes, nor clamor to get at the work. We offered two Saturday workshops on our own sponsorship, leading less than ten women each time through the clogged passages of thinking that weighing more than normal means we are unattractive. Occasionally, we would interest a church or women's organization in sponsoring a workshop in order to reach new audiences. We wanted to find, and provide a gathering place, for those few women brave enough to give up dieting or be large in a thin-obsessed culture.

Most women consider it easier simply to conform to what our culture demands of us—that we work to match the narrow, random, irrational, ever-changing window of female attractiveness with constant dieting, denial of food, 12-step programs, exercise not for health but for slimness, surgery on our bodies, and makeup and clothing that approximate another's idea of sexual attractiveness, plus anything we can do to cover up those evidences of aging—white hair, face wrinkles, and heavier and differently shaped bodies.

Most women in these classes were smaller than size 16, worried about getting larger, thinking they are fat at size 12. Although they knew well the worth of freeing themselves from the prison of societally sanctioned attractiveness, many still think there's a magic road to self-confidence and health—*and most deeply believe that being thin is an essential part of that path.*

We always liked the work, but at some point gave it up. Linda needed to concentrate on full-time work, and marketing our work would take more time than either of us were willing to commit. She and I meet occasionally to catch up on each other's lives and for me to gain insight from Linda's attendance at Overeaters Anonymous and to learn from the difficult time she went through when her best friend—both of them beautiful, talented, competent, large women—joined Jenny Craig.

A year ago, I decided to lead a six-week journey through "Women, Weight, and Appearance" at a community college, and designed each week's two-hour class as we went along, although working within a general framework.

With each class or workshop, I realize what keeps me returning to the work: I do this hard work in the last third of my life for Jane, my sister who died at life's two-thirds mark of 60. I really do it for me, but I wouldn't know about how women suffer for the cultural shame of being large if it weren't for her, my part in the abuse of her, and if I hadn't become "heavy" in late middle age.

Jane and I could call it genes if we could find some fat ancestors. Actually, my paternal grandmother, divorced from my grandfather, was fat. Mother was offended by thrice-married Mabel Shumway Raymond Peddle Laidlaw's presence on her few visits back to Nebraska from California to see her son Jack and his family. She was fat, sloppy, and colored her hair with red henna dye, wore costume jewelry and bright colors, and had a bosom that nearly spilled out of her dresses. Her appearance, not even considering her fallen-woman status, was distasteful to my mother. I can remember sitting on her lap, feeling all that fat through my mother's revulsion.

Except for our enormous repugnance toward Dad's mother, we glossed over any heavy or large women ancestors. Mother's mother, I remember, was certainly not a thin woman, square and stout in her housedress and apron.

There were some hefty *male* ancestors. Do their genes count? In today's climate, the people abused because of how much they weigh, or don't weigh, or how petite or large they are, are mostly women, and not so often men.

To my knowledge, my mother never weighed more than average. I certainly don't remember *her* dieting. But *I* remember dieting, talking about weight and size, and acting as if any girl or woman heavier than my mother and we three girls was somehow lesser than us, not in control of their appearance, which we considered an affront to us and unseemly on their part.

There was mother's special friend among Dad's "girl" cousins who was always heavy, and we loved her; I do not remember any criticism of her in my house. Mother's own cousin Helene, a strong, tall, large, newspaper woman in Wyoming, was never called fat by us or spoken of disparagingly because of her weight and size. There was the vegetable lady, Mrs. Steidly, who arrived at our front lawn, produce spilling out of her car as she spilled out of her old house-dress. I remember no comments behind her back after she and my mother negotiated fruits and vegetables, bushel baskets full for canning, smaller amounts for supper. She was confident in her world of farming and selling as my mother was in hers of superbly managing our house and her family.

I do remember a faint amount of self-righteousness that we felt toward another family, which was based on our thinness and size, my mother and we three girls, based on their family's inability to achieve that exalted position.

The issue was undoubtedly control. But on the surface it read that the worst thing you could do was to become "overweight." Actually, not coping—and not being extraverted—were probably right up there with any slight dalliance with fat. Yet, I remember the teenage, family-sanctioned ritual of coming home after dates to fix a big sandwich in the kitchen before checking in with our parents in their bedroom. We would make big sandwiches on white bread, slathered with mayonnaise, and filled with bologna, tomatoes, lettuce, and cheese. Food was seen as closure, as bonding, as relief.

None of us were fat, although middle sister Ann and I, the baby, were a little chubby in our early teen years. Oldest sister Jane, five foot ten inches tall, had a 22-inch waist as a young woman, we bragged.

Jane married, had four babies in quick succession, gained weight and kept it on, and was easily considered a "large," "heavy," or "fat" person. For the rest of her life, which ended at age 60 after a valiant three-year struggle against cancer and its dubious cures, she was fat and *defined by that in my family.*

On long-distance calls to my mother, "How is Jane?" meant only "How much does she weigh? How does she look?" Over the years, Jane went on various diets, several at someone else's urging. Mother always reported this good news.

To this day, I have no memory of ever wondering how Jane felt about all this, nor any report from anyone about how being heavy affected Jane. I do not have to ask how such abuse affected her.

One time, Jane went faithfully to a special diet program—I think the Diet Center—where every day, she weighed in and got lots of support for her efforts, and lost weight. I remember that mother bought Jane new clothes as a reward. Mother occasionally bought Jane clothes "to help her" look thinner, tidier, slimmer, more socially appropriate, in Mother's eyes, in the eyes of all of us who have internalized the rules of our surrounding culture. Today I keep doing the same for myself—randomly buying clothes in which I hope I can see myself looking nice, different than fat, most efforts rather unsuccessful.

After the months on this new regime, Jane gained the weight back and more, predictably as I understand now. The family line was, in mother's words, to commiserate with Jane's husband: "Poor Bud. He paid all that money and now she's heavy again." I doubt that we ever said it right out, said "fat." Euphemisms and clothing to cover pounds were everything.

After Jane died in 1988, I began to consider my own part in that abuse. I rarely asked "How is Jane?" to hear about her life, her kids, her joys and sorrows, but rather asked only as shorthand for "How much does she weigh and what does she look like?"

Such is karma: looking at myself in the mirror today, and for several years, I see my sister Jane, her white hair and her large body. Only it is me, and I still see her/me with those eyes that judged and criticized Jane.

One time, going through photographs at Jane's house, I was surprised to see her tall and smiling, proud to be honored for her courage in continuing to attend national conventions of an organization her husband was president of. She went in spite of her worsening cancer, sometimes in a wheelchair, in spite of wearing wigs, and, the last time, still large, her gray hair, grown back in curly, long and as beautiful as she, cascading over the shoulders of a stunning dress. These photographs showed me a sister I never knew—a proud woman, a brave woman, a woman who knew her worth and ultimately, I hope, her beauty.

I suspect that in families everywhere, we are both known and limited by our relative's definitions of us. Jane was the eldest, middle daughter Ann and I were more conventional children. Jane dared to exhibit anger; in our family, such overt expressions were reserved for our father. We said with patronizing, slightly disapproving smiles that Jane always brought home strange friends, strays who needed love. Jane didn't stay at the university long enough to be initiated into her sorority; instead, she came home and got married, "too young" we said in those days. "A rebel" we called her, the label for anyone who set one foot off the path delineated by our parents, that middle-class, middle-American, small-town, bourgeois life.

Jane must have seen a broader life, having to carve out a place for herself with anger, with a kind of dominating overconfidence, with a reverence for the myth of the upper-class family we pretended to be. So we focused on what she looked like, constantly urging her to become one of us, camouflaged in thinness and conventional manners, instead of cherishing all her differences.

I look and look and look at heavy women everywhere and think they look wonderful. I love their clothes, their bravery, their ability to go about in the world not covering up their size nor appearing to be ill at ease for breaking the social code.

Sitting at an outdoor cafe with a friend this spring, I was startled to hear her criticize the appearance of a woman who walked by our table. Over the years, my friend has seemed not one of those caught in the "I am what I look like" trap. Here she was, she and I both old women now, saying she didn't like what another woman looked like. I told her I thought the woman and I looked alike—a slightly heavy woman wearing a purple long skirt and matching T-shirt, similar to my outfits, except for that day. As a guest at that same friend's luncheon gathering, she informed me ahead of time that so-and-so "has just lost 35 pounds and looks wonderful." The dieting woman announced at the table what everyone except me seemed to know: "Your stomach determines your dress size." I toyed with my silverware and tried to change the subject.

Another old friend whom I see infrequently burst out "Look how awful that woman looks!" as we drove by a bicycler with a safety helmet on. Again, I could only respond, "That's what I look like when I ride my bicycle."

Both friends were, I think now, trying to ignore that I have clearly moved into the fat-and-old-and-therefore-unattractive-by-societal-standards category. They hope to cover up that knowledge by criticizing other women in front of me, as if I were still in the game. Or maybe they were trying to let me know that I had let go of being "attractive" and am now subject to the criticism of other women, including themselves. Who else but large women, in this culture, have to go through such analysis and angst over casual remarks that hurt, to justify insensitivity!

I find happiness when I am not at all concerned with what I look like and think I look just fine, no matter what clothing I have on, or what my hair might look like, or what makeup I have not put on—at suppers in church basements, in community with other social justice activists, at Quaker meetings—but never, never, when I am dressed up and out in my traditional milieu of white middle-class heterosexual couples. Even there I find heavy women and marvel at how wonderful they look, how easily they carry themselves among others. I want so to be able to know such beauty and confidence and ease for myself. I remember Muriel, that extraordinary friend of some time back who called hair "just head covering" and said she dressed each day in "whatever in my closet wants to be worn."

I pray for my radical self-consciousness to go away. I mourn my sister Jane, clearly and regularly abused for her differences by her family of origin. Jumping over my own pain, I bolt into anger, anger at myself for ever buying into the "you are what you look like" lie, for taking such a long time to get over it.

So I do the work, this work for Jane—my sister Jane, big-hearted, friendly, goofy, angry, dominating, lonely, opinionated, helpful, generous; my sister Jane, a good friend, hard worker, TV soap opera addict, wife, mother, grandmother, musician, seamstress, and much more than I could ever see. I never saw her beautiful body, her lovely clothes, her mischievous smile, her pensive face, through my own terrible prejudice.

She might have forgiven us our cruelty. I wish she did not internalize it. But I know she did carry the criticism within herself, even though she fought to be herself against a system that says you're okay as a woman only if you fit some random, irrational definition of what is attractive.

Rest well, Jane. I want this work to be some sort of amend. A true amend, to you as well as to me, would be to love my body and love what I look like, to love us both in the mirror.

Chapter 4

Who Do I See in Another's Eyes?

The first time I gave a talk at a meeting of Alcoholics Anonymous, which was a big deal for me only one year into recovery, I said "I have always defined myself by who I saw in your eyes. Whoever you wanted me to be, that's who I tried to be."

Back then, more than 20 years ago, I spoke in the past tense, thinking that to see myself only reflected in someone else was over. I assumed that not drinking alcohol or taking any other mind-altering drugs suddenly made me totally real, vulnerable, present.

The road to recovery offers those possibilities along its excruciating exciting path, but, as the old song says, "It ain't necessarily so!" which reminds me of a delightful poster that reads, "The truth will set you free but first it'll make you miserable."

Not only have I internalized what this culture says about heavy, old women, but I am daily able to project that internal script onto my husband. My friend Nan used to remind me that the world is full of hooks for my projections, none of them an excuse for my not claiming my own stuff.

If I think I am beautiful, would that make him think I am? If I am still—at my age!—struggling with what I look like after several years of being heavy, do I find that same dislike of my appearance in him? The fact of the matter is that my appearance has changed. I have been heavier than average for several years, and it is sometimes painfully obvious to me that my husband no longer sees me with approving eyes.

I got fat one time before this, nearly 25 years ago. During the worst years of my active alcoholism, I ballooned from the good-old size 8 or 10 to beyond 18. Except for bathrobes, only my lovely camel wool pantsuit still covered my body. It began to look so stretched that I had to find other clothes at the nearest department store. I have no memory of shopping, only of having three outfits: one a blue polyester afternoon dress that looked terrible on me; another a cotton jumper (photographs of me wearing it in a parade make me wince); and the last, a polyester white evening gown and a matching jacket to hide my stomach, to wear to the White House.

We have photographs of that occasion, that dress-up night at the White House. One is of my husband in his fancy tuxedo, and another is of me smiling, trying to pretend I thought I looked okay. Actually, when I look at that photo today, I think I look perfectly alright, nice even, except for thinking I didn't. That whole year I bore the pain of old and new friends exclaiming that I was pregnant, followed by my struggle to allay their embarrassment and hide my own shame.

That night of the White House function, I later learned, my mother called my children at home to ask what I looked like when we went to the White House. I do not know if her concern was whether my alcoholism or my fat was showing. I'd guess she wanted to know what I looked like, concern over my obvious alcoholism relegated to second place. In our culture, alcoholic behavior is forgiven if we don't get drunk, cause scenes, slur our words, and not behave in socially inappropriate ways. We pooh-pooh it, saying things like "She may drink too much sometimes but she certainly doesn't have a problem." Even to be drunk, in places where excessive drinking is not only tolerated but encouraged, is often more acceptable than not drinking.

That White House night, my children felt bad for me, and tried to assure their grandmother that Mom and Dad went off looking swell.

Even now, more than 20 years later, I remember knowing that my husband was ashamed of me, from what he did not say and the look in his eyes, ashamed that I was now fat and that the dress I had shopped for so ignorantly was only barely acceptable for the occasion.

On another equally painful occasion, one bizarre summer, I endured my husband's judgment and dismay of both my alcoholism and my fat, seeing it clearly in his face, his body language, his eyes. We didn't talk about either "dysfunction," though he occasionally urged me to drink less, covered up for a drunk wife, and never mentioned my size, except indirectly. In our pathetic attempts to pretend and to avoid the pain of facing our troubles, we continued to live together as man and wife, that behavior seemingly easier than changing or speaking out loud the truth of our increasingly difficult lives.

I know that we humans project our emotions and thoughts onto others in our lives, yet there is a certainty in recognizing another's emotions in their posture, their eyes, their facial expressions, their gestures. We accept quite easily from one another reports that someone is "cold," "affectionate," or "upset," all of these moods conveyed without words. Especially telling is silence when affirmation, verbal or physical, or some response is obviously appropriate.

Thus, I do not doubt my perception of that "look" in my husband's eyes, that look that, without words, reflects the thought process of not liking the appearance of a heavy woman before him, that woman who had been mostly trim, well-dressed, and an enthusiastic participant in the establishment most of the years he had known her.

A lot of the details of those difficult times I have managed to forget and have no desire to dredge up. Yet, now that I am again and for the rest of my life heavy—besides old—I keep trying to block out what I perceive in his facial expressions and in what he does not say. "You can lead a horse to water, but you can't make him drink" well describes my random attempts to encourage him to tell me I look nice.

Aldous Huxley, in his old age, recommended only that we become kinder to one another—the accumulated wisdom of his long and intellectual life. One of my rules for living in community is that we frequently and lovingly tell each other how wonderful we look, always, always finding one positive thing on which to remark about when with someone, preparing to go out with them, greeting them, being with them.

One of my deepest behavioral characteristics is attempting to get my emotional needs met from the place or person least able to supply that. I call this behavior the "random rat" theory; that is, if I get random affirmation, I line up every time hoping it will happen again. If someone regularly affirms me, I can relax and trust that regularity, without begging or pawing for it. My husband pleads that he is only concerned with my health when he mentions my size, my eating habits, checks my girth in a new dress or outfit. I tell him that is patently untrue.

I doubt that it was concern for my health that awful night years ago when he moved away from me and refused to speak, except when necessary, the entire evening at a reception. Coming from a week at a Writer's Conference, I had stopped at a highway discount mall and bought a skirt and top for the cocktail party supper that I thought would make me look okay. I was steeped in days and nights of hanging out with other women, all of us writers, focusing only on writing and having a great good time. I knew the minute I saw the other women in satin evening suits that what I had on was woefully inappropriate; not dressed right and heavier than the other wives, I stood out like a sore thumb.

The next morning, I insisted we discuss his behavior; it did not go well. This was the first time he fell back on insisting his concern about my weight was only concern for my health. We had several other such painful, angry talks throughout that week, I remember, only days later able to move on together in any kind of love or acceptance.

I knew it was not concern for my health when my husband of more than four decades grabbed a bag of potato chips from my hand, which he and one of our daughters were sharing as we watched a video at midnight on New Year's Eve, 1995. He expressed disgust that I continued to eat potato chips after he had stopped. Lamely, through terrible hurt feelings, I told him he was not in charge of what I ate. "I guess not!" he yelled, an unmistakable reference that if he were, I would look different. I've long hated New Year's Eve and this particular one was no exception!

We finished the evening, him trying to say goodnight as if nothing had happened, me in such psychic pain I could hardly function. Meeting a friend and her new partner for tea the next afternoon, I could only cry, seeing no way out or through the paralyzing, painful fog that engulfed me. That eruption of our differences kept me isolated and in pain for six straight days, my gentle reference to the explosion a beginning way out and to a new place, for both of us.

I want to emphasize that my husband and I have come into a kinder old age in the last year or two, and that we are better than we used to be. He has slowly grown used to who I am and what I look like, heavy and old. He knows that I am an even more valuable person today than that wildly ambitious young woman he was attracted to a long time ago. I have come to some nonchalance about my weight, size, and appearance, am occupied nearly full-time with writing and leading workshops, and doing work in peace and justice communities, somehow more able not to demand approval or permission from either a person or the world.

W. Charisse Goodman, writing in *The Invisible Woman: Confronting Weight Prejudice in America* (Gurze Books, 1995)—a powerful no-nonsense book—minces no words as she asserts,

> Weight can also serve as the focus of a power game between men and women, with husbands and lovers grumbling in a martyred manner about the "little woman" having "let herself go" and never letting her forget that she has not fulfilled her part of an unspoken bargain. It may be easier for her to play along with this nasty game than to risk defying other people's expectations, especially since this attitude is broadly reinforced by society. . . it should come as no shock that . . . the women who oppose these dictates are treated as hypersensitive harpies and humorless shrews. . . The fact is that the deeply ingrained tyranny of weight prejudice is really just another way for a male-dominated culture to define women in terms expedient to the ruling class. . . she must constantly struggle simply to be at peace with her own flesh. But as long as women spend years of their lives and billions of dollars torturing themselves with diets, as long as they yearn wistfully for the promised magic of liposuction and the cosmetic surgeon's knife, or risk their health, even their lives with questionable diet pills and experimental weight-loss surgery, *society raises no real objections* (emphasis mine). (p. 76)

Goodman also describes a woman

> who actually suffers from the adverse effects of weight prejudice and who protests the attendant social injustice (which she is more than qualified to describe) cannot be taken seriously because she could only be a bitter, ugly loser who couldn't get herself a man—exactly like the ridiculed suffragettes described earlier . . . the "battle of the bulge" being a more acceptable preoccupation than uprooting comfortable assumptions. Where

weight is involved, rejection is understood to be the thin person's sole prerogative, and a fat woman is considered a beggar, not a chooser. (pp. 78-79)

Quoting Shulamith Firestone, Goodman's fierce book reports,

For the exclusivity of the beauty ideal serves a clear political function. Someone—most women—will be left out. And left scrambling, because as we have seen, women have been allowed to achieve individuality only through their appearance—looks being defined as 'good' not out of love for the bearer, but because of her more or less successful approximation to an external standard . . . If they don't, the penalties are enormous; their social legitimacy is at stake. (pp. 88-89)

My good friend and therapist Janet Waage Lingren, EdD, tells me that "There have been times when I have met a couple for the first time and my impression of the woman is that she is very attractive, only to discover as we talk, only to hear her husband say 'She used to be a beautiful woman but she let herself go,' referring to the fact the woman weighs more than she did in her youth."

Jan calls this situation in her couples counseling "not unusual . . . I have also heard it from the women, that their husbands are critical of their weight. The sexual relationship has diminished or ended, he is no longer sexually attracted to her because of her weight."

"I have to avoid saying or showing," Jan advises, "that [such an attitude] really makes me angry. I tell the couples, the husband, that is it important that you focus on what you value in the person and realize that we all change as we get older. That is not a reason to no longer love or be sexual with the person."

In her years as a therapist, Lingren reports, "I have heard men say that they love and value [their partner] for her many qualities and then say, 'I don't know what I would do if she ever got fat.'

I think they're afraid they won't have an erection, they are afraid of losing the sexual dimension of life, afraid they won't be attracted to her, not ever having the experience of having sex with a woman who is less than ideal in her weight."

"Can men change their attitude?" I asked.

"Some can, some can't, some won't," she answered in a quiet voice.

Every once in a while, I go places where who I am is just fine, even when I have taken no care to "look nice." My middle-class self is clean, clothed at least presentably, and my hair brushed. Last Sunday, I came happily home from our Friends Meeting first-Sunday-of-the-month pot luck, having had my usual wonderful time there, talking with people who also do not dress up as the world does. There my self is free from the poison of wondering if I look alright and judging how others look.

I go about erranding and grocery shopping in old sloppy clothes, but have told myself the old gray sweat pants with holes in the crotch may no longer go out of the house, nor may I go clothes shopping in jeans or a sweat suit.

I take care how I dress for leading workshops, teaching classes, or giving talks in front of groups, and *always* see at these events women heavier than I am who I find delightful to look at, well-dressed, and obviously comfortable in their bodies. I absorb the ambience of such women, loving how they look, admiring their courage in not dressing to hide their shape or size, and still looking lovely.

Sister Jane never tried, that I know of, to change the abuse of her family of origin. We also never complimented her on how she looked, that I know of. Perhaps Mother and Ann did, especially after some makeover of Jane via a new diet or good clothes.

What other places do I feel affirmed for who I am and can drop my obsession with my appearance? At all peace and justice gatherings; at any pot luck supper in someone's home or a church basement; sometimes as I go walking but not always, visible as I am then to passers-by. Surprisingly, at the swimming pool where other old, heavy people swim laps, I am at ease with myself, though not so surprisingly, since we're all in the same boat, or pool, there.

I love to listen to Carolyn Heilbrun talk about this journey into a new land, one in which our partners must accompany us "either in love or alienation." We would not be judged on age or appearance if we had just been appointed to the Supreme Court, she suggests, and offers that powerful image for those of us struggling with this new stage of life. When Dr. Heilbrun was still on the faculty at Columbia University, she would sometimes attend the first faculty meeting of the fall term without wearing her name tag. "They thought I was the cleaning lady," she reports, laughing. After she put on her name tag, they (other faculty) snapped to attention, rightly suspecting she might be voting on their tenure.

There is substantial research on fat prejudice and discrimination: in hiring, in promotions, in salaries, in getting grants, in acceptance to graduate school, even in being waited on in stores and restaurants, and in theater and airline seating. Old women know well their invisibility, unless our bulk arouses someone's ire, gone past our culture's measure of sexual attractiveness, past being needed.

Since I am assertive, I have known less of such behavior. I have lived in this town a long time and am well-known. People have probably gotten over saying to one another "Did you know she's gotten fat?" but I haven't let go of thinking that's what they are saying, especially if I meet someone I haven't seen in a long time. Why do I think my size is the object of anyone's interest or conversation? The paranoia, and the brutal reality, of the out-of-step in this culture.

In the midst of all this discussion, I am aware of veering off onto other subjects, avoiding who or what I figure my husband sees when he looks at me. I would not think of asking him what he thinks, considering myself an expert reader of body language after so many years of training. I no longer present myself as a target for someone else's "honesty."

Years ago, during a time when I was fat and desperately sick with the disease of late chronic alcoholism, I bumped into old neighbors in the concourse at O'Hare Airport. The wife stopped me and said she wanted to tell me something, "because I love you." She looked over at her husband and said "because we love you, don't we, dear." That was back in my "target" days. I smiled sweetly and listened to her tell me of her concern for "that beautiful, brown-haired woman you used to be," and wonder about "where she went?" Idiotically, I thanked her, said I'd think over what she said—What? decide how best to hurt myself more?—and walked away, having taken an enormous direct hit to my gut. I was angry for years, telling anyone who would listen how awful it was. Finally, I stopped that. I use one of the six filters for criticism that I learned from my old beloved teacher Sidney Simon (*Negative Criticism*, Argus Communications, 1978) who says you have to stay around long enough to pick up the pieces if you criticize another. A hit-and-run attack on another does not qualify. I also tell people in my classes to "run for your lives when someone says they are going to tell you something because they 'love you.' "

Those whose lives are connected to ours, who stay silent instead of affirming us, who say nothing and project disgust, help us to be similar to all oppressed people and to police ourselves. I have even become careful about how I let my husband see me, never intentionally standing sideways in front of him with the full extent of my stomach visible, so I do not have to see him looking me up and down, or able more easily to notice my fat stomach sticking out. This is as self-defeating as wearing clothes that I think cover up or diminish my size. I am strongly aware of the dysfunction of accepting another's view of myself to describe my identity, of the idiocy of giving over my self-respect to someone who I know is caught tighter than I in the narrow appearance rules of our culture.

Men are severely limited by the culture's demand that their eyes become beacons searching only for attractive—that is, slim and young-looking—women. If you are a grandmother, which I am not; or a caretaker of children or old people, which is not required of me at this point in my life; or Mother Teresa, of whom there is only one; you may look old or heavy, being unfashionable not a moral failing. Only those three categories and their attendant duties, those projections of others, give women release from the strict codes of what we are to look like.

Men are denied the ability to love and be friends with all kinds of women, especially those men who are caught and choose to stay caught even when help is offered, in the briar patch of what constitutes attractive. Their lives would be richer by outgrowing, throwing off, or learning past the idiocy of feeling good about themselves by having a "babe" to show off and validate their importance and virility. This would open doors to a more vital old age for both men and women, even if that "babe" is the first wife, over 60, skinny as a rail, hair dyed, and not harmonizing with one's skin color anymore, expensively clothed, and face artfully made-up.

Renowned African-American writer and philosopher Adolph Reed, Jr., writes in the August 13, 1996, *Village Voice*, in "Have We Exhaled Yet? The Black War Between the Sexes,"

If you try to live without a man, unless you're part of a statistically small minority fortunate enough to be financially independent, you wind up either impoverished or facing a constant grind to avoid impoverishment. If you marry your way into contingent economic security . . . your dependence is your ticket. This becomes clearer with time, as you experience erosion of the two main features on which your spousal position rests when men have the resources to choose and women are objectified—youthful attractiveness and novelty. Thus the specter of the suburban matron who starts freaking out with the first wrinkles and goes on to support the growth of a vast cosmetic industry—from skin care fads to personal trainers to the physical mutilation of plastic surgery—in a desperate battle to, as Cher so aptly sings, hold back time.

He concludes,

In this context it's exceedingly difficult for men and women to form personal attachments that are not tainted by the lash of the market. Engels was right: healthy and honest attachments are scarcely possible under patriarchal capitalism. The fact is that we have no idea about what a family form worth valuing would be for our society and can't until we overcome gender inequality. To that extent, whatever works for individuals freely choosing is what's right.

As I struggle with all these surface issues connected to the deep roots of cultural attitudes toward women, I am glad to come upon such writers and thinkers who provide historical, social, and political analysis. The bedrock work of such people grounds and steadies me, while it expands my own mind.

I hope to live long enough to be free of external standards of size and appearance, and to have a healthier internal definition of appearance. Women are socialized to remain powerless by concentrating on what we look like, all the while leaving men to run the world. It does not please me that I am so long ensnared in this trap.

Maybe Capricorns, as my husband is and mother was, are stuck on outer appearances. My mother was critical of me, overtly in her case, and of my husband's girth on one occasion I especially remember. I was shocked and saw him wince when she commented about his size when she met us at an airport. I want to live from the knowledge that everyone is on the path they need to be on and that I can learn to step aside and move past immovable objects. I must learn to constantly be grateful for this healthy, strong body that serves me well.

For the rest of my life, I must concentrate on valuing my life, my past, my work, my friendships, my ups and downs, my choices and decisions, the road traveled in my 65 years (one less traveled for the past two decades). I *must* value my thoughts, my size, my laughter and anger, my connections, my dreams and causes, my depression and anxiety, my good days and bad days, everything that makes up this infinitesimal brief dot on the planet that is me.

Audre Lorde wrote in "Age, Race, Class, and Sex: Women Redefining Difference," from *Sister Outsider* (The Crossing Press, 1984, p. 123), this wisdom I am terribly grateful for:

> For we have built into all of us old blueprints of expectation and response, old structures of oppression, and these must be altered at the same time we alter the living conditions that are a result of those structures. For the master's tools will never dismantle the master's house. As Paulo Freire shows so well in *The Pedagogy of the Oppressed*, the true focus of revolutionary change is never merely the oppressive situations that we seek to escape, but that piece of the oppressor that is planted deep within each of us, and that knows only the oppressors' tactics, the oppressors' relationships.

To value my rich life and my Venus of Willendorf figure is a demanding call to action and reflection in these final years of my life. I am glad I am paying attention, not feeling, as poet Marge Piercy writes in "If They Come in the Night," "that I forgot to do some little piece of the work that wanted to come through." I wouldn't have missed it for the world, even though I did not choose it, often wish it would go away, am in danger of appearing foolish (god forbid!), and only awkwardly make my way along this strange path.

Chapter 5

Tucking in My Blouse

Today I am at home writing. I have done an amazing and wonderful thing for myself. I have spent the day with a T-shirt tucked *into* my jeans, not hanging out, not carefully pulled over my stomach, not rolled up over, but *tucked into* my pants, no sweater or shirt covering up that "indecent" protrusion by hanging below my fat waist.

You who have never been a fat woman will not understand. You who are more self-accepting about your size will scoff. You who are a good shopper will give me advice. You who are graduates of the don't-make-a-fuss school will be slightly annoyed.

At about noon I noticed a role model in my head. It is my childhood best friend, who I saw last at our forty-fifth high-school reunion. A practical woman; matter-of-fact; full of humor, good cheer, and common sense, she evokes enormous admiration in me each time we've met as adults. She did so especially at the reunion barbecue, where she looked happy and stylish in western jeans, boots, and a handsome white shirt *tucked in*! She even had a belt around her not-thin waist.

I think I wore something to hide my girth, probably slacks with a light sweater or T-shirt hanging out, wide enough at the bottom not to delineate my bulging stomach. "Why can't you be like her?" my extremely thin sister asks, "She looked wonderful tonight." I thought she did, too, but it took enormous self-confidence and lots of chutzpa on her part, I thought, not to try to disguise her size. (I must say though, that I heard that weekend the same sister who advised me to accept myself, commenting along with other people on people's size and appearance privately, among themselves, after a luncheon, or the dinner, or the brunch. Usually such comments were about people they hadn't seen for a long time and were mostly voiced by still thin women.)

Who do I think I am kidding, going around in loose tops over slacks and skirts? Such outfits only make me look bigger, probably. I am smaller in naked person than I look in any clothing I own. Perhaps that is true of all of us. When I cover my slightly expanded behind, much fuller bosom, and pregnant-looking stomach in some loose thing, I do not look slender, not fat, thinner, or anything of those ghastly goals one is socialized to approximate in one's clothing.

So, here I am today, writing, occasionally emptying the dryer, eating lunch at my desk. I sort through some loose ends, but mostly write, happy and productive with my shirt tucked in, my fat stomach obvious.

It really doesn't look so bad, I tell myself, looking in the mirror at this unusual sight of myself. In fact, I am rather pleased that I look *less* fat than if I had a loose top hanging over these jeans. But only in my own eyes, I know.

After all this work, I still think I see people looking at my fat self with disapproval. Junior-high young people report searing self-consciousness as they turn away from the food line in the school cafeteria to find a table; I re-lived that adolescent feeling intensely in the cafeteria dining room at a treatment center for alcoholism in the fall of 1977. Again I feel that same self-consciousness in these strange years of experiencing old age *and* a different body. I walk rapidly downtown, as if to give others less time in which to determine my size. In the winter, under heavy coats, who can tell anyway? An exercise used in a treatment program (see Chapter 19) focuses on, among other things, freeing fat women from their reluctance to appear in public by assignments to do just that. The 51 women in that program became more revealing of their bodies in public. Daniel Goleman reported in an article from *The New York Times* news service, published in the April 3, 1995, *Lincoln Journal*, "One woman, preoccupied by the fatness around her neck, for example, started to wear her long hair pulled up rather than covering her neck."

I *might* risk going about in public, obviously fat, in a belted dress, shirt tucked into skirt or pants, or form-fitting (oh, no!) dress or sweater. If I did this at least once a week, say, I could see if that behavior manifested cumulative ease about myself. What a risk!

When I gained weight, I didn't ask anyone's advice about how to dress. Looser and bulkier regular-sized things undoubtedly made up my wardrobe. But after I got over wondering why clerks in good dress stores looked at me unsmiling and said sharply they didn't have anything for me, and finally found large women's dress stores and departments, I kept on covering up the fat, layering it with long tops over bottoms. I've never known that place below my waist where the top should end gracefully. I suspect that I emphasize my stomach's furthest perimeter by wearing tops that stop right there. I am too short to wear long tunic tops, but keep buying them to try anyway.

American women, maybe just middle-class white women, grow up knowing how to look at themselves in mirrors, hoping to see less of themselves, hoping the dress they are trying on makes them look thin, slenderizes, as we say. My eyes are my mother's. We know all the tricks, we who are the other, the looked-upon. I have read that black women in the United States diet less, that information surely connected to economics as well as culture. For an entire population of people, imported across the middle passage and kept in tortuous slavery and then second-class citizenship, to be told to become less in order to meet an external criteria of acceptability must surely seem a bad joke, if not evidence of the insanity of the culture they live in.

Today has been fun, so great to have my body back. I actually have my own body back when I can feel my stomach pressing against the waist of my pants. Imagine, I have a waist, even if it's not one that is smaller than my bottom or my top. Who said a waist had to go *in*? Who said we are not supposed to feel good in shorts or bathing suits IF WE ARE FAT?

I keep thinking of the lack of self-consciousness on the part of my old childhood buddy. Could I be brave enough to do as she does, to stop the useless and idiotic attempts to cover up my fat, to try to look as if I weighed less than I do? Then, perhaps, I could adopt some of the traits of that person I so admire—she who is always glad to see me, cheerful, full of humor and good sense, and strong enough to accept the world as it is and not tear herself up fighting so much, as

I do. Actually, I think it's genetic—my old friend is herself and I am myself, too; but I'd like to have some of her ease with the world, her lack of cynicism, her gentleness with herself.

Freedom may await me at our fiftieth high school reunion, where anyone who is still alive and able to travel and face social functions will have given up any judgment about what others look like, given up anything but laughing at younger pretensions. The old bogeyman, for women, of *the high school reunion* will have faded away, leaving us at last to be only and wonderfully ourselves, grateful to be alive.

This day of practice has certainly helped. I may do it again soon. But in front of others whom I know are judging as they look? I don't know about that one. Courage is what we need to grow old in this country, to grow up into our real selves, all our fur rubbed off by then, our stomachs happy to be sticking out, no one telling us to hold them in.

Chapter 6

There's Good Work Out There: What Others Are Saying

There are days when I want to go through my life handing out leaflets.

I have much experience "leafletting": downtown weekly for years in front of the Federal Building at 7:30 a.m., with our Central American Response Team, against the U.S. policy in Central America; annually on tax day downtown with a War Resisters League flyer showing where our federal tax dollars go; four times yearly at each local high school with my Alternatives to the Military Committee and a flyer titled "Questions to Ask your Military Recruiter"; early in my marriage to my political husband, handing out Republican literature at the door of a school district meeting, for which we were kicked out; and an occasional "leafletting" or "tabling" in Boston\Cambridge with daughter Anna.

What I want to hand out now are the copies of brilliant work being done by women, and some men, deconstructing the cultural edict against fat and large women. Often I am tongue-tied or simply too angry to tell people how I feel. I want to explain that what I am often inarticulate over is backed by much more eloquent and extensive scientific opinion, research, and data, and speaks to the relentless attack on women who deviate from the cultural norm in this country. When I get angry, trying to explain the nonsense of yet another myth about fat people, I see others smile smugly, as if to say "For god's sake, will she ever get over her anger?"—a way of dismissing what I am struggling to express.

Susan Kano's *Making Peace with Food, Freeing Yourself from the Diet/Weight Obsession* (Harper and Row, 1988) is absolutely the best book I know of for people seriously interested in recovering from the size/weight/appearance obsession. Kano demonstrates quite thoroughly in this excellent blend of research, information, work-book pages, and step-by-step self-help, that genes, metabolism, and lifestyle are the main determinants of weight and body size.

She encourages readers to

> reclaim a natural way of eating that respects their body's hun-ger signals, to accept, and yes, even *love* their natural size and shape, to celebrate the joy of movement in dance, exercise, or sport, to value *who* they are (not just what they look like), and to feel as good as they can feel and enjoy life as completely as they can. (Preface, pp. xi-xii)

Making Peace with Food is filled with strategies for inventorying one's history and one's current behaviors. Kano insists that *"We must undermine the causes of our preoccupation* by eliminating those we can eliminate, and learning to live with those we cannot." (Chapters 23, 24, and 26 include more of Kano's work.)

In *Beauty Secrets: Women and the Politics of Appearance*, by Wendy Chapkis (South End Press, 1986), "Jean" writes, "We are all brutally oppressed by the people who package our fears and sell them back to us. The culture is so permeated with it that it is hard to step back and see that."

Chapkis' analysis explores the links between appearance, gender, and sexuality; empowers women to share the secrets of their rela-tionship to imposed standards of beauty; and shows how women are constantly required to "pass" by wrapping their "unacceptable" and "undisguised" selves in layers of conformity to acceptable beauty standards. The analysis looks at beauty and ugliness, racism and beauty standards, and the role of class and economics in shaping images of beauty.

I need to reread books such as this to remind myself of what I know, and to help myself grow beyond feeling self-conscious and lacking in self-confidence because I no longer fit the young and thin category. In my obsession, I do exactly what the "beauty myth" is designed for—spending a lot of time, money, and emotional energy trying to be "attractive" even though larger than I used to be.

Sociologist Becky Thompson speaks of "hunger both in the physical sense as women's need for food and metaphorically as women's hunger to experience our bodies as sacred and powerful, our appetite for creative work, and desire for access to our fair share of the world's resources" (in "Women's Hunger and Feeding Ourselves" in the fall 1988 issue of *Women of Power*, a splendid women's publication that went out of business in the summer of 1996). Thompson more recently authored *A Hunger So Wide and Deep: American Women Speak Out on Eating Problems* (University of Minnesota Press, 1994).

Feminist writer Kim Chernin tells us in *The Obsession: Reflections on the Tyranny of Slenderness* (Harper, 1981, p. 110), "In this age of feminist assertion men are drawn to women of childish body and mind because there is something less disturbing about the vulnerability and helplessness of a small child and something truly disturbing about the body and a mind of a mature woman." (Chernin, unfortunately, intimates that weight is the result of some disorder, not just an ordinary fact of life. For example, she speaks of women pushing vital longings into the unconscious, which later manifest as obsessions, and writes, "when the fat woman begins to acknowledge the feelings that drive her to eat, the body begins to express this knowledge, takes on the flesh it requires to mature, and *gives up* [emphasis mine] those pounds it has been using for the purpose of avoiding feelings.") I still consider her work strong, truthful, and full of courage.

Thompson again speaks plainly,

> In the U.S. this image is upheld by interlocking institutional powers—an eleven billion dollar [increased to $33 billion from 1988 to 1995!] reducing industry in which 95% of the consumers are women; a medical system which maintains the dubious assumption that fat is by definition unhealthy and needs to be eliminated; a multibillion dollar advertising industry which markets a race, class and age-biased model of beauty; a job market in which women who do not fit this model of beauty must deal with discrimination; as well as an insurance industry that penalizes those who do not maintain the medically prescribed image of what constitutes a healthy body size. (p. 78)

Essential reading also includes Susan Faludi's *Backlash* and Naomi Wolf's *Beauty Myths*.

Even though Wolf now says that "Feminism lacks positive imagery" in her new book *Fire with Fire: The New Female Power and How It Will Change the 21st Century,* plus many other complacently commercial and patriarchal statements, she authored one of the finest articles of those I collect, in the *Voice Literary Supplement* of December 1989. In "Hunger Artists: Women Starve at the Meal of Fortune," she writes one of the most powerful analyses of women and food I had ever come across. She wrote presciently in *The Beauty Myth,* "A cultural fixation on female thinness is not an obsession about female beauty but an obsession about female obedience."

Wolf concludes the *Voice* article with the following:

> For women to sustain self-denying attitudes toward food means that for them, during these holidays of life-affirmation, there is literally nothing to celebrate. . . . The Pilgrims might have made it to the harvest, but plenty or not, for women it's still going to be a long hungry winter. The lamp may have lasted for eight days, but all it illuminates is the unfilled plate, sign of the barren earth.
>
> As long as women are made to bring the anorexic mindset to the holidays, the communal table will never be round, with men and women seated together passing the dishes, but the same old hierarchical dais of eating, drinking men, with a rickety folding table at its foot.

The *Voice Literary Supplement* then gives a list of "Edible Complexes": in *Fat Is a Feminist Issue* by Susie Orbach (Berkeley, 1978), Orbach sees women's shapes as expressing their conflict about their society, rather than seeing that society has a conflict about women's shapes; In *Never Too Thin: Why Women Are at War with Their Bodies* by Roberta Pollack Seid (Prentice Hall, 1989), Seid writes that "The 1959 insurance tables that fueled the weight hysteria are based on bogus science; thinness is no correlate for health, and the cause of most eating disorders is simple: the body's reaction to the physiological stress of dieting, or semi-starvation"; and in *Fasting Girls: The Emergence of Anorexia as a Modern Disease* by Joan Jacobs Brumberg (Harvard University Press), Brumberg reports that "Her thesis cuts closest to the political bone:

the disease begins as a response to the pressure of a culture of thinness" and "advanced capitalism depends upon the derangement of appetite—especially women's." Ah, at last, the bottom line.

I heard Professor Carolyn Heilbrun speak in the late 1980s in Lincoln, Nebraska. After much effort I obtained a tape of that talk, still surprised it did not receive wider distribution or publication. In that speech, which was condensed in the *Smith Alumnae Quarterly*, Summer 1991, she takes apart the "male gaze" under which most women live.

"Signs of age," Dr. Heilbrun asserts, "come upon women in our society like marks of the devil in earlier times. And it seems we must fight them, fight by painful and irreversible acts upon our bodies, or allow ourselves to be captured by regret, resentment, and despair." She describes Simone de Beauvoir in her fifties, sixties, and seventies:

> Instead of trying to recapture the old life, designed in the hope that men would look on her with desire, she moved into the new world of age, where her voice, her ability to affect events, increased. ... moved from anger and aging to the discovery of a new life. . . she allowed herself to be transformed, not by plastic surgery, or the infusion of silicon, or the removal of ribs or fat, but by looking to another country [the future] where they do things differently.
>
> As she ages, a woman must escape, if and for a time, in camouflage, from that [male] gaze. . . . Men will still say, if I am not turned on by just looking at you, you are no longer woman. And she will answer, only youth has that talent, and I will not impersonate youth. I will not live in drag for your sake.

Heilbrun exhorts us to drop "that baggage of the male gaze, the fear of disappointing people, the anxiety about not being dressed right, the knowledge of not seeming desirable."

Writer and nurse Sallie Tisdale addresses and examines "A Weight that Women Carry: The Compulsion to Diet in a Starved Culture" in a long essay in the March 1993 *Harpers* magazine. Among other brilliant, brave things, she says,

In trying always to lose weight, we've lost hope of simply being seen for ourselves. . . . The fat person's character flaw is a lack of narcissism. She's let herself go again. . . . Fat is perceived as an *act* rather than a thing. It is antisocial and curable through the application of social controls. . . . My thin friend assumes my fat friend is unhappy because she is fat: therefore, if she loses weight she will be happy. . . . By fussing endlessly over my body, I've ceased to inhabit it.

Many women wrote to *Harpers* to applaud the Tisdale article, and to share their own fat oppression and fear. Claudine Denman of Hawaii, however, writes (in the June 1993 issue),

"Let the fat whiners eat cake, but tell them to keep their pudgy arms off the armrests at the symphony; their knees out of the leg space at the movies; and their girth out of my paid-for airline seat. In fact, let's request handicapped space for our plump friends. But for God's sake, charge them for the larger chairs and bigger aisles. Then those of us who *are* able to resist an extra mouthful won't feel squished as we sit delicately in our little spaces.

Whoo! Poke the skunk and get sprayed!

Sallie Tisdale responds in the same issue to this and another critical letter that equates being thin with simply balancing calories with exercise, and eloquently writes that "With few exceptions, to diet is to put image—*surface*—before kindness, wisdom, and joy." Punishment of both fat women for being big and fat men for being soft is "for violating the arbitrary requirements of gender, which are intrinsically political, as are all the elements of homogeneity in a society. . . . Hatred of female bodies is deep within us, surely. But even deeper is a fear of all bodies, of the imperfect and unpredictable flesh itself."

I recommend care in reading or hearing about a new book or approach to women's appearance. Many current weight-loss programs and surgical groups usurp words from feminism, as if they were the ones offering true liberation and increased self-esteem, instead of body loss and rearrangement.

The issues of aging and appearances are twined, I think, since both large women and women older than whatever age anyone else considers worthy of attention, are ridiculed, discounted, dismissed, made invisible, or criticized that they do not please the gaze of the looker.

Cynthia Heimel, one of my favorite writers and a woman willing to speak the truth, once wrote the following in her "Tongue in Chic" column in the January 18, 1994 *Village Voice* a stunning answer to a woman who wrote in to The Problem Lady (Cynthia) complaining about her mother—"bonkers," "nose stuck in everything, the insistence on omniscience!": "Your mother is constantly being smashed in the face with the fact that she is not only useless but invisible . . . and when she's not invisible she's ridiculous. . . . Come on, who really needs the support group here?" (p. 37). Hurrah for The Problem Lady!

I read *Radiance*, a powerful, life-affirming, beautiful magazine for large women, in addition to anything I can get my hands on that points out, stands up for, and joins us on the way out of the beauty myth. I want to tell the world, especially people who disparage fat and large and old and different, all this good news so conveniently ignored in the mainstream media.

Kip Tiernan, "irreverent stalwart of the Boston social justice community" and founder in the early 1970s of Rosie's, the first shelter for homeless women in the United States, remarks wisely in "Interview: Social Justice," to writer Mark Andersen in the May 1996 *Z Magazine*, "The terms of the debate are set by those who profit most from the conclusion."

Among the articles I hand out to classes is Dr. David Garner's basic work on the effects of dieting in "Rent A New Thinner Body?" in the winter 1991 *Radiance*; Cynthia Rich's comprehensive "Agism and the Politics of Beauty" from the March-April 1990 issue of *Broomstick*, a radical magazine for older women, which is no longer published; "The Radical Ideas of Jane Hirschmann and Carol Munter," a review of Jane Hirschmann and Carol Munter's *When Women Stop Hating Their Bodies* (although these women continue to use the prejudicial phrase "overweight"), by Susan Lawrence Rich, in the fall 1995 *Radiance*; "The Fear of Fat" by Marjorie Nelson in *Broomstick*; "Transforming Body Image," an interview with Marcia Germaine Hutchinson by Carole Biederman in #18 *Women of Power*; "The Code Women Live By . . . When We are Good, We are Very, Very Good," by Claudia Bepko and Jo-Ann Krestan in the June 1990 *Moxie*; and "Integrating Disability Studies into the Existing Curriculum: The Example of 'Women and Litera-ture' at Howard University" by Rosemarie Garland Thomson in the #47 issue of *Radical Teacher.*

Several of the books I recommend whenever I am teaching classes about Women and Weight, are (including those mentioned here and in Chapter 2) the following:

Real Gorgeous by Australian Kaz Cooke (W. W. Norton, 1996); *Where the Girls Are: Growing up Female with the Mass Media* by Susan J. Douglas (Times Books, Random House, 1994); *Women En Large: Images of Fat Nudes*, with photographs by Laurie Toby Edison and text by Debbie Notkin (Books in Focus, San Francisco, 1994) in which, amidst the splended photographs and poignant writ-ings by the models, Notkin writes this succinct, powerful sentence: "Perhaps worst of all is the total near-lack of any kind of cultural reinforcement for transforming the pain into anger, or political energy, or even acceptance"; *Breaking all the Rules: Feeling Good and Looking Great, No Matter What Your Size* by Nancy Roberts (Penguin Books, 1987); *Shadow on a Tightrope: Writings by Women on Fat Oppression*, edited by Lisa Schoenfielder and Barb Wieser (Spinsters/Aunt Lute Book Co., 1983); *For Her Own Good*, by Barbara Ehrenreich and Deirdre English (Anchor Books, Dou-bleday, 1978); *Overcoming Fear of Fat*, edited by Laura S. Brown and Esther D. Rothblum (Harrington Park Press, 1989); and *No Fat Chicks*, by Terry Poulton (Key Porter Books, 1996).

Reading is a source of enormous comfort to me *and* the route to a new freedom and a new happiness. Barbara Walker's *The Crone* changed my life. I read to shore up my courage and self-esteem when the culture I live in tells me large women are not worthy unless we fit in, measure up, go along. I consider each new book or magazine/newspaper article a message making its way through the prison bars, helping to set me free from both the cultural prison and my own internalized self-hater, as Starhawk so wisely labels that critical inner voice (in *Dreaming the Dark: Magic, Sex and Politics*, Beacon Press, 1982).

Chapter 7

I See My Insides/You See My Outsides

"All they could recognize of you were your beautiful blue eyes," my friend told me, repeating a mutual friend's reaction to seeing me at a funeral.

Why did she have to tell me that? I wonder today.

Way back then, at the funeral of a beloved fellow alcoholic, one whose return to drinking may have precipitated the aneurysm that caused his death, I was heavier than I'd ever been, wearing terrible clothes, in the final year of chronic alcoholism, and struggling every minute to appear normal. She was probably telling me, in no uncertain terms, how ugly chronic alcoholism had made me.

She and I went to lunch after the funeral and had a nice time together. I did not drink at lunch that day, and we were glad to be able to comfort one another over our friend's death.

I guess for someone looking at you, their only guide is what you look like. But these were people whom I had known a long time. And I was still what I looked like: "her blue eyes were all I could recognize."

This week, listening to a favorite jazz program on the radio, I was shocked to hear Preston Love call Della Reese "obese," the only subject he chose to address about this elegant, renowned jazz singer. He said, "She let herself go, she doesn't take care of herself. There's only one reason to get obese and that's from eating too much. I am nine weeks into my diet and controlling eating is all there is to it."

So, Della Reese, long an acclaimed musician and admired person, is only what she looks like and fat is not acceptable to her fellow jazz artist Preston Love. "Let herself go," "eats too much," and "obese" are words we hear often about women who have become larger than size 12, the legendary male gaze's outer limit of attractiveness, I would guess. (The illuminating correspondence between Preston Love and me is discussed in Chapter 20.)

Trying to "get up" emotionally for my first high-school reunion since I got fat, I was sharing my fears with my therapist. She reflects back a much healthier self to me than does my own mental critic. Finally, she reported about herself, "This is who I grew up to be," suggesting that I take that stance with old high-school chums who would notice my changed body.

"This is who I grew up to be," and you can take it or leave it! covers the entire person, not just what someone else thinks I look like. Here, however, I have fallen into the trap of insisting we consider the "true" beauty of a person, not based on their outer attractiveness or ability to follow the cultural commands to thinness, instead of what I know is the more important work of broadening what we consider beauty, including both inner and outer manifestations of that.

Why is not the lovely, voluptuous fat body of Della Reese beautiful? How can Preston Love acknowledge the beauty of her music, her life, her soul, and still not see any beauty in her body?

For those old friends at that funeral, only my blue eyes were left of my former beauty. My body was unacceptable, my unfashionable clothing was offensive, the color of my hair was not right. Not even could they not see me as a person worthy of affection, but were very clear that their judgment of my appearance was the main issue of who I was that day. I certainly would have settled for them still liking me, even in the face of that rejection of what I looked like.

Cynthia Rich gets it exactly right in "Agism and the Politics of Beauty" in the April 1990 *Broomstick*. Here is the final paragraph of that excellent article:

I am looking at two photographs. One is of Septima Clark, on the back of the book she wrote in her late eighties about her early and ongoing work in the civil rights movement. The other is a postcard of Georgia O'Keeffe from a photo twenty years before her death. The hairs on their scalps are no longer a mass, but stand out singly. O'Keeffe's nose is 'too' strong. Clark's is 'too' broad. O'Keeffe's skin is 'wizened,' Clark's is 'too' dark. *Our task is to learn, not to look insultingly beyond*

these features to a soul we can celebrate, but instead take in
these bodies as part of these souls—exciting, individual, beau-
tiful (emphasis mine).

Recently, I came upon *The TEEN FACE Book,* a question-and-answer guide to skin care, cosmetics, and facial plastic surgery, prepared by the American Academy of Facial Plastic and Reconstructive Surgery. What did I expect? But I plowed ahead and read, with growing horror, placating words about "looking different's not all that bad" immediately followed by much discussion of the "option" of facial plastic surgery: "If your nose doesn't fit your face . . . . If your chin is weak or your mouth is small . . . . If your eyes droop or look angry . . . . If your skin has scars, moles, or birthmarks . . . . If your ears stick out . . . . If your cheeks need bones."

This thinly disguised promotion piece for facial surgery on teenagers plays on young people's fears of not fitting in and young women's need to be considered attractive by their male peers. The before-and-after pictures emphasized in photographs and words how changing one's face via surgery helped one to be more confident, increased self-esteem, and was noticed favorably by all. "Student delighted with chin surgery"; "Lips: is 'pouty' better?"; "Sometimes mother does know best" (recommending nose surgery to her 13-year-old); "Nebraska teen gets nose surgery for her birthday"; "Nasal surgery or chin implant?"; "Excess fat under the chin: liposuction can help"; "Bags, circles, and other eye problems"; "Why do I have these ears . . . and what can I do about them?"; "Ear surgery turns tears to smiles"; and on it goes for 184 pages, concluding with "Put your best face forward."

Sure, plastic surgeons have books about plastic surgery in their offices. Yet I find this particular book particularly exploitive of teen insecurities through its offer of facial surgery as a way to deal with life. Many of the photographs and some of the text emphasize serious physical problems, such as birth marks and accident scars, but the major thrust of both text and photographs is to show how much better your life will be after surgery on your face.

It was long ago that a group of my women friends listened to one of us report back from her initial visit with the facial surgeon. What

I remember is that he warned (did he warn?) her that most of his patients got a divorce within six months of obtaining a face lift.

I admit it's a struggle, being human and fat. Even thin people think they are not beautiful. People with disabilities or midgets or people with scarred bodies or faces really know what it is like to have people get past what they look like, to see who they really are. But are not our fat bodies, our skinny bodies, our short selves, our wounded bodies, our diseased bodies just as worthy of respect? Are we all the "Elephant Man," a beautiful soul hidden within a misshapen body, being derided for that and needing to hide ourselves?

In *With the Power of Each Breath: A Disabled Women's Anthology* (Browne, Connors, and Stern, Cleis Press, 1985), I found this beautiful meditation introducing the book's fifth section, titled "This Body I Love, Finding Ourselves" (p. 246). Although it is written for "disabled women," I take the liberty of substituting "fat" or "old" each time the word "disabled" is used. In no way do I mean to diminish any of the deep, true, and painful struggles of disabled, or differently abled people, by coopting this powerful writing. The editor's work, her words, do fit, however, for both fat and old women, also wildly discriminated against. (As a matter of fact, this section introduction is immediately followed by a scathingly honest and painful life story by Carol Schmidt, titled "Do Something About Your Weight.")

> Our bodies are our most precious and often our only possessions. They have also been the recipients of such tremendous pain and anguish that many disabled women have dissociated our bodies from our "real" selves. Our bodies have been the targets of medical abuse. We have been hospitalized and have spent years in doctors' offices and still our bodies have not cooperated. Some of us live in chronic pain, some with chronic unpredictability and others with chronic stares. We have felt the deep personal invasion of surgeries and endless diagnostic procedures. Sometimes we feel as though our bodies are trying to kill us. They betray us in our struggle to resist patriarchal desires for "feminine weakness."
>
> We need to see our bodies as worthy parts of our selves in order to invest the time and energy it takes to care for our-

selves. Society works directly against this possibility. We are regarded as "defects," as women with something "wrong" with us. Specialists trained to treat one or another of our body parts have contributed to our dismembered body images. Value judgments are assigned to our "good" and "bad" parts. Health is seen as a virtue, disease as evil and ugly. Our integrity as persons has been undermined.

Feminine beauty is manufactured by cosmetic and fashion industries and changes seasonally. Our self-worth suffers when we respond to this sexual objectification. Disabled women have been excluded from patriarchal conceptions of beauty and sexuality. Again, we are encouraged to see our bodies and our selves as distinct. Our beauty is reserved for the inside. Inner beauty is used by our culture as a consolation prize for those it finds ugly. Symmetry, clear eyes, straight limbs and fingers, uniform pigmentation and smooth motions are prerequisites for outer beauty, no matter what else may be popular. People jeer at us. We may not be able to find appropriate clothing for the outside and are advised not to call too much attention to our "flaws" with bright or fashionable adornments. Prostheses, canes, hearing aids, wheelchairs and braces are not designed with aesthetics in mind. Our individuality is not encouraged or appreciated.

We claim our bodies and our integrity as disabled women. We insist on our right to make informed decisions about our bodies. We do not have good parts, bad parts, or inner beauty. We come in many sizes, shapes and colors. Our bodies deserve our love, tenderness and pleasure. We are whole, beautiful and sexy women!

What a rich, real portrait and affirmation of *ALL* women.

When you stop to think about it, what qualifies for beautiful, on the outside? Sharon Stone at the Academy Awards? Elizabeth Taylor at 19? Helen Hayes at 80 or Jessica Tandy at 85? Jane Fonda, her exercised and surgically shaped body on Ted Turner's arm? Roseanne at her funniest? Radical Emma Goldman? Anthropologist Margaret Mead? Feminist scholar Andrea Dworkin? New Age guru Marianne Williamson or health faddist Susan Powter? Trophy wife

Georgette Mosbacher? Author Naomi Wolf who now thinks that "feminism lacks positive imagery"? Betty Friedan? Marabel Morgan? The "gorgeous" ones get the jobs, the attention, the publishing contracts. Are they better for their adherence to the LOOKS rules?

A not-so-secret weekly reading in my house is *The National Enquirer.* My husband and children used to buy it at the grocery store, as much for its voyeur stories as to hear me huff and puff about how low-class it was of them to read it.

Now that I read it, I know what a conservative magazine it is. Even on the page of colored photographs of famous women at some recent public event, *The Enquirer's* values predict who looks good and who doesn't. Most of the time, they applaud sexy outfits, unless they don't like the woman in question and decide she's looking too sexy, that is, her mini-skirt is too short, overblouse too see-through, or, naturally, she is too old for such an outfit. The old women, hair dyed, makeup artfully applied, bodies skinny and curvy from exercise and surgery, such as Joan Collins, always draw raves. *The Enquirer* likes women who scrupulously follow the culture's edicts, including those about clothing, body size, hair style, colors, shoes, jewelry, and attitude.

Inside I am both a nice and a not-nice person. I hope others see mostly the nice side of me. Sometimes, I avoid looking at my whole body in a mirror in order not to have to listen to that inner voice who reminds me that I am fat and old and who equates that to being unattractive. We were brought up, however, to know that looking at our reflection in a mirror or store window was wrong, egotistical, vain. I don't understand why only my size 10 self was worthy of commendation, even from myself, especially since I know that the person I am now is a whole lot more real, honest, and wise than that thin and young-looking middle-ager I used to be.

"Beauty in things exists in the mind which contemplates them," David Hume wrote in the 1740s. Later, Margaret Wolfe Hungerford, in her novel *Molly Bawn,* wrote, "Beauty is in the eye of the beholder." Of course, we bring to everything we see our selves, our prejudices, our moods, our genes, our experiences. So why cannot all we beholders widen our eyes to the beauty of all sizes, shapes, and kinds of bodies, even those to which the male gaze reports no subsequent erection?

Once I sat in a recovery meeting in a small town in Nebraska. I knew no one there and felt uncomfortable being there. I didn't see a soul I thought I liked. As each person spoke in the traditional format for 12-step meetings, his or her face changed in my eyes. It was as if a light followed each speaker, illuminating and making human, and therefore beautiful, each face. Only my fear and dis/ease kept me from seeing every single person in that room as beautiful. The minute we shared the commonality of recovery from alcoholism, and we spoke out of our deepest lives and wounded hearts, I saw each person differently.

We should all have such experiences and be open to their life-changing possibilities. May we be as willing to face the truly ugly realities of prejudice, as does the woman who speaks for disabled women, and to overcome them, both personally and politically, within and without.

May I continue to enlarge my sense of the beautiful, starting with my old, heavy self.

Chapter 8

The Lifelong Diet

I got the award that year, I remember. It was presented at the regular Monday morning meeting of Weight Watchers, which I'd attended for several months, from December 1985, until May 1986. The award, a shiny metal key chain, was emblematic of my weight loss from 151 to 133 pounds. It read "key to the future" and I believed it was indeed that.

My goal had been "to get down to" 130 pounds and I felt bad about not reaching it, perfectionism at work I suppose. The "counselors" at Weight Watchers were not at all disappointed, telling me that perhaps I needed to revise my goal to the more appropriate 133 pounds for my 5'5½" frame. (The other day I found my old "attendance book" with its weekly weight listing, loss or gain recorded, stamps affixed for each week's weight-in and class. It makes me sad, this tarnished emblem of an inflated sense of power, of a linear march toward something special and better, at age 54 grasping for thin and therefore still attractive.)

Little did I even suspect that this victory in Weight Watchers was the beginning of the end, the end for me of being thin, of that halcyon time of not thinking of or feeling the need to cover up my size with clothing, of being able to see myself in mirrors or photographs without wincing. I had spent my life in a schizophrenic bind—constantly thinking of my size and weight and semi-consciously knowing I looked alright, at least certain *I* was not one of *them*, the women who were chunky, fat, large, obese, sloppy, plump, chubby, flabby, corpulent, thick, broad, portly, pudgy, porky, wide, overweight, heavy, stout, matronly.

The old joke, to which I once gave laughing assent, was to hear a woman say, "There's a thin person trying to get out of this fat body" in response to anyone daring to suggest that she had a "large frame" or "big bones" on which to drape too much flesh.

My friend Linda tells of being taken to the doctor by her mother, at age eight, for diet pills. That story horrifies me, yet I think back to the constant attention as I grew up to one's size, to what we weighed, to appearances. That emphasis on appearances, although absolutely normal for that time of the 1930s, 1940s, and 1950s, surely was exaggerated for us in our "Dad is sick" (but really addicted to codeine) household. We had to be better than other people, and had to look as if nothing were wrong.

My mother, in that household of two parents and three girls, was extremely attractive—that's how we would say it then. Without saying it out loud, we were proud of her, proud of how pretty she was—and who she was—that pride a bond among me and my sisters. By the time she died, bravely, at my sister's house, her white permed hair surrounding her sleeping face like a halo on the pillow, I found her more beautiful.

We didn't exactly diet but, like everything else in those days, our eating was closely monitored. "Going on a diet" consisted of eating lots of carrots and celery for snacks. We always ate "well" and "sensibly." Right before the birth of my first child, Ann Leslie, I remember, my weight and blood pressure went up, so the old carrots and celery snacking plan was put into effect by my mother.

Photographs show my sisters and me in various stages of baby fat and early teenage body plumpness. Oldest sister Jane was the thinnest; we bragged for years about her 22-inch waist and her shining dark brown hair. Middle sister Ann and I were blue-eyed blonds, shorter, and the same body type. Ann and I were chubby little things, outgrowing all those stages to be reasonably attractive teenagers and high-school cheerleaders.

So ignorant, so self-inflated were we, so callous of others was I, that I wrote a psychology term paper in junior college on the inferiority complex, an old psychological term, using as models of dis/ease and lack of self-confidence two very fat women in that small school. As I might have known, had I been more conscious or even compassionate, that paper, or rumor of it, reached them. I can hardly bear the memory of my stupidity, my arrogance, my obvious superiority complex.

My father died when I was a senior in college; after his memorial service, I returned to the University of Nebraska, 500 miles from my hometown, to take finals, and then went back to Scottsbluff to spend the three-week semester break with my mother. What I remember about that time in January, then already thinking about marrying a young lawyer with whom I'd had one or two dates, was that I got a permanent, received a fancy gray wool suit from one of mother's rich friends, *and* lost ten pounds. I was ready for a new life, one without my sick father, and one that included the possibility of marriage to that lawyer, politician, older young man. We were engaged by Valentine's Day. The all-too-obvious parallel of those two men was lost on me until years later. I acted out unconscious issues

By the time I was married, staying thin was a virtue, a conscious act. Disappointed at not becoming pregnant in the first five years of my marriage, when all my college friends already had babies, I determined to be the most outstanding anything, including best-looking, by being the thinnest. I did not become anorexic or bulimic, but quite strongly adhered to that suspect reasoning in my mind.

Later, I took diet pills, ever so lucky not to have become hooked on them, even though I can remember that lovely burst of energy I got at eleven o'clock each morning when I took the day's pill. A strange moment of sanity broke into my life the day I dumped my remaining diet pills down the sink, scared I would become addicted to them, as my father had been addicted to codeine, from which he died at age 50. I have nearly forgotten all the diets on which we bought some special powder to mix with milk or juice that substituted for breakfast and lunch, being assured that we were getting all the nutrients we needed without food.

In the days when I was at home with children and was an active Junior Leaguer and socializer, I remember one particular week's dieting in order to look terrific for a party that weekend. I did not eat anything all day Saturday before my husband and I drove to Omaha to a house-warming for some friends. I wore a fashionable white sheath dress and quickly joined "the boys" in drinking 9-to-1 martinis, kept in the freezer so as not to dilute them with ice cubes. By the time someone suggested seeing the new house, I had to crawl from room to room and thought it not entirely unusual, only amusing. It took us a long time to drive home, stopping frequently for me to throw up. For the next two weeks, I could only leave the house long enough to pick up my children at nursery school.

Daughter Mary thinks that my purposeful vomiting, whenever I was nauseous from too much alcohol, borders on bulimia. This is the daughter who, at 5'11", and going through puberty, became slightly chunky, the sight of which was commented on often by her father as she would enter a room where he was sitting. He voiced what I suspect I too was thinking. Too bad neither of us ever had at least a biology lesson about the bodies' needs during puberty, much less the slightest sense about how to nurture a child through those difficult adolescent years.

I have recovered from commenting on people's appearances, especially of women's weight, shape, size. Yet I make a point to tell especially old and large women how beautiful they look. My husband has not given up considering what he thinks women look like as a strong indication of how well they are doing, so socialized and conditioned to that ultimate compliment, and remarking yet on his daughter's slim figures as they appear at Christmas in our living room. When he calls another woman attractive or comments in some way on her appearance, I ask him what that is based on, "That she is thin?" I demand. He pleads innocent to noticing. (A woman physician I met at an Iowa Writers Workshop told us about her experiences with patients, in which the husband finds the now-heavy wife unattractive and then focuses on his slim daughters, both to compliment and be attracted to, and to demonstrate to his wife the error of her appearance.)

We all talked about our diets, my friends and I, all the time. Refusing desert or not taking a roll, we didn't have to tell one another we were dieting, but someone would ask, in order to give the dieter an opportunity to feel good, to be praised, to be smug about her will power. Men were not included in these discussions; at least I had no margin for hearing them, consumed as I was in women's size and shape. The irony is that we were including them in all these discussions since staying thin, staying in shape, not letting yourself go, were for attracting the gaze of males and the praise of peers.

Our conversation naturally included *the* greatest compliment we hear and give, beyond all others: "Oh, you look so wonderful. You must have lost weight." Second best is the infantile, "Which one is the mother and which one the daughter?" How we praise women for "not aging."

The act of losing weight is supported nearly everywhere in our culture. Women report that they diet "not to lose weight but because I feel better when I weigh less." Who wouldn't, as we get compliments and encouragement from every source in our lives, even unconsciously see that body in the mirror or store window reflecting what our deep socialization tells us is one of the highest values?

We are advised to hold in our stomachs, that place of power, of stability, of the solar plexus. Of course a woman holding in her stomach becomes less powerful physically, less able to claim her space, physically off balance. The ancient Venus of Willendorf goddess statue is not our model, she with the round, heavy, forceful belly. I love to tell groups of women that no one ever told that goddess to "hold in your stomach!," one of the main instructions girls hear and young and old women adhere to rigidly.

Even though I don't remember specifically, I suspect I sounded like the women I hear in the locker room at my swimming pool, always, always, always talking about what they weigh and what they eat or don't eat.

Women equate eating and growing fat with sin:

"Oh, I was naughty last night."

"Isn't that desert just sinful!"

"I have to pay this week for what I ate over the weekend."

"The holidays are so hard; I suppose I can redeem myself after the New Year."

Listen to women in a locker room, at their swimming pool, at the buffet table, in front of desserts. Henry Jaglom's *Eating*, a film about women at a birthday party in Los Angeles, paints a devastating portrait of women and their socialization and status concerning eating and size. Perhaps Jaglom meant his film to be ironic, since only these upper class women have the luxury to *NOT* eat, and to constantly obsess about their size, weight, and appearance. Worse than that, one might consider, is watching those women judge and rank each other according to some insane, random, ever-changing, invisible standard of size and shape. We become the enforcers for our oppressors.

Watch a woman weighing herself, her face an amazing mix of trying to look unconcerned but registering her dismay, grief even, at one or two more pounds, and her unlimited joy at the loss of same. Even the skinny ones.

I was the typical American woman, dieting, dieting, dieting, obsessing about food, obsessing about my looks, my shape, my weight, my size, my clothes—and ready to tell you that I did not occupy my life with those things. Maybe I still am. I always felt a little fat; nothing is good enough when one inhabits a body that takes up space, needs energy, gets sick, absorbs not only carcinogens but cultural edicts not to exist, at least not in any other way than a way pleasing to others.

Sometime in the 1970s, our family doctor and neighbor in Arlington, Virginia, diagnosed me as pre-emphysemic. I quit smoking for two weeks and gained weight; I immediately started smoking again, not only because I was severely addicted (two to three packs a day for years) but because I wanted to stay thin. I made the choice between a life-threatening breathing disorder and being attractive, choosing attractive over life. Yet in my mind, I blurred those obvious choices in order not to have to face the insanity of my behavior.

The last diet was that addiction to Weight Watchers. I loved the weekly meetings, with the pretty, confident woman talking to us about how to achieve victory over the scales. I bought the tiny scales to measure ounces of food, but was never very faithful about recording my food intake. I persevered, cheering for every weight loss, feeling superior to women who certainly had more to lose than I did, and reveling in my weight loss.

My usual breakfast of cereal and fruit sat beside me in the car those Monday mornings of the Weight Watchers weekly meeting, right there so I could eat the minute the weigh-in and cheering session was over. I always wore something light, no jewelry, and took off my shoes to be weighed.

After those weeks of faithful attendance at Weight Watchers, I weighed 133 pounds and was a heroine, a victor, a winner. There began my weight gain. My body had endured one more starvation and would respond appropriately: gaining back enough to make it through another starvation siege, which means more than I had lost. The last weight I recorded was 175 pounds; now if I have to board a small plane and estimate my weight, or on the driver's license test, I put down 180. I have not looked at a scale in years, and am no longer tempted to know what I weigh, as if that were the worth of me.

Many new studies show that yo-yo dieting itself causes enormous physical problems for a body, besides the eventual gain of more weight.

So unconscious was I for years that I did not consider it inappropriate that an acquaintance went to Duke's "Fat School" and had his jaw wired shut in order to lose weight. Nothing was too bizarre to accept for those of us obsessed about what we weighed, what we "looked like," for those of us smart enough to stay attractive.

When I began that journey to the Weight Watchers club room each Monday, an analyst I saw infrequently felt it was not a good idea, "unless you are doing it for your health," she cautioned. Of course, I assured her, I was doing it for my health and not for sexual attractiveness.

She knew well the trap set for women in this country, which I was stepping into voluntarily: lose weight and the world is yours— romance, men, travel, riches, clothes, admiration, adulation, beauty, confidence. None of that is true, especially the trap of promising women, ever so subtlety, that losing weight will make them attractive to men, we who are automatically receivers of the approving, disapproving, or ignoring male gaze.

It seems odd that we keep dieting, keep trying, thinking that to starve ourselves, to weigh less, to become smaller, offers what we think our lives are missing. Or that after one diet, women don't catch on that they are being lied to, the myth that losing weight will assure them a great man or at least somebody, and that everything that is wrong in our lives will suddenly come right by losing weight. How odd that we do not see through that sickening deception, which offers the illusion of control to the "second sex."

In *The Beauty Myth,* Naomi Wolf calls dieting "the most potent political sedative in women's history; a quietly mad population is a tractable one" (p. 187). I read her sentence over and over again, marveling at its succinct wisdom, its exact description of dieting.

William J. Fabrey, in his Spring 1995 "Big News" column in the magazine for large women, *Radiance*, quotes many experts in the field of nutrition, eating disorders, and psychology who now emphasize "the possibility that psychological and physical damage from weight cycling might be greater than the risks of obesity." He reports on proceedings from a National Institutes of Health conference, whose summary reported that "obesity should not be targeted in young people or citizens of any age, *and may not even be responsive to intervention of any kind without causing eating disorders or lowered self-esteem*" (emphasis added) (p. 28).

Fabrey is a director of the Council on Size and Weight Discrimination and a member of the National Association to Advance Fat Acceptance (NAAFA), which he founded in 1969.

A weird backlash to the council's sure knowledge, in Fabrey's words, that "*diets fail, not the dieters!*" surfaced in an April 12, 1992, *New York Times* story titled "A Growing Movement Fights Diets Instead of Fat." The new emphasis on accepting all shapes, sizes, weights, ages, colors, body configurations, and differing abilities, which is strongly encouraged by the size acceptance movement, was quickly labeled as a troubling anti-diet movement. The press informed us that various persons and groups noticed with shock that a bunch of weirdos are suddenly against diets, insinuating that such a position is for no good reason!

The evidence on dieting is that it increases weight. Dr. David Garner, former director of research in the Eating Disorders section of the Department of Psychiatry at Michigan State University, reports that "cultural pressures on women to conform to a gaunt Twiggy image of physical attractiveness [was] a major factor responsible for the incredible surge of eating disorders in the 1970s and 1980s. It has also become apparent to me," he continues, "that many women developed horrible conditions such as bulimia as a result of 'successful' treatment of their 'obesity,' and that the real culprit is dieting" (*Radiance*, Winter 1991, pp. 37, 42).

He continues, "Weight loss is relatively easy in the short run, but maintaining the loss is very unlikely. . . Body weight fights against deviation from its preferred levels, and this process operates for people who are heavy, just as it does for those who are thin." Not facetiously, Dr. Garner says, "You can rent a new, thinner body, but owning it is a completely different matter!"

He warns against the health risk factors of dieting, such as "hypertension and elevated blood lipids . . . depression, anxiety, irritability and social withdrawal . . . and a profoundly negative effect on self-esteem."

Calling the $30-billion-a-year diet industry (now $33 billion) "snake oil of the worst variety," Dr. Garner refutes the mortality fears of higher weights:

> One study indicated that there was no difference in mortality risk for women of average height who weighed between 115 and 195 pounds, and those who weighed more or less than these weights had a mortality risk that was still lower than that for a man of average weight or less! . . . There is evidence that health risks associated with weight do not necessarily translate into higher death rates. . . Research on the health risks associated with *dieting* suggests that weight fluctuation may be much more dangerous than simply being heavy.

One more time: American women are fed a myth from every source available in order to assure us of the high value of becoming who someone else wants us to be!

Yet I am not free of this insanity either. There are still nights I go to bed and mornings I wake up thinking: If I just did sit-ups every day, I wouldn't have this protruding stomach; and if I exercised more than the 45 minutes a day I faithfully do, maybe I'd lose weight.

Having been brought up to understand deeply that I could affect anything I wished to, and that such was my job, I think I can reverse the effects of aging, that I can become more conscious *and* stay chained to mainstream opinion, that at least I can control what I look like, especially to random others.

No, my journey led me to quit dyeing my hair, to stop dieting, to stop wearing shoes with any elevated heels, and now it asks me to stop obsessing, fussing, and spending energy and money on what I look like. Part of that journey's difficulty is that I live, we live, in this belly of the beast, this culture and the internalized voice that says I must "keep myself up" and "not let myself go," that to show my age and weigh more than the average are issues of moral laxness.

I am healthy, I am old, I am conscious, and I live among people who diet and talk about their diets all the time. At a peace potluck last year, I expressed my displeasure to the people at my end of a table that their conversation had gone on boringly long, as they compared diets and foods and weight losses and gains. When they thought that was funny, and kept on obsessing about their weights and food consumption, I got up and left the table, maybe afraid I'd join in their socially approved conversational subject, no longer willing to pay attention to our obsession with what we weigh. I was slightly put off by the dissonance of talking diets in a roomful of activists gathered to hear of the desperate conditions of most Nicaraguans.

No Overeaters Anonymous for me, no "Gray Plan" for my eating, no such thing as abstinence, no sponsor to talk to. Yet I do not binge or purge, as intentional vomiting is called, nor put more food in my stomach than it asks for at a sitting. Only fat people assure others that they are eating "good" food, still replying to the unsaid comment about one's size with assertions of one's healthy ways. At least for me, this new life of not dieting and learning to accept myself as just perfect the way I am this minute is another one of those roads less traveled, of which one discovers many in middle and old age.

Chapter 9

What's Funny About Fat?

One of the things I want to do before I die is develop a better sense of humor. I think it will help me endure the exigencies of getting old, besides those I have experienced thus far.

So I think to explore humor in relation to being fat, it seems inappropriate in the extreme to pair the two subjects—in the case of humor and fat, humor and aging, only gallows humor suffices— except that I am of the opinion that humor makes things holy and conversely, that nothing is too holy not to laugh about. A friend who writes to me of her discomfort with pairing humor and fat, tells me that "what you want to do before you die is to feel comfortable with humor in relation to being fat."

People make fun of and tell jokes about fat people. Sniggering is what I think people do behind our backs. I *know* some do, those like my formerly superior self who viewed the world from her size 8-10 self, that wonderful, acceptable, "aren't I doing it *all* right," size.

Beyond sniggering is the destructive gossip that passes as humor. This past week I was horrified and stunned to hear what was currently circulating as something funny among the socially elite in my town. On an upcoming yacht trip to entertain politicos, the joke was that the large woman, sister of the host, and a large male national commentator were to be placed on opposite sides of the yacht to balance their weight. Women know on whom that joke rests.

Only my shocked face hid the tears of pain overflowing my eyes as I listened to this bon mot carelessly repeated. Later I cried again, telling my husband that no one deserves that kind of treatment, that just because "everyone does it" is hardly an excuse for meanness and cruelty. I cried for all of us whose physical appearance becomes the butt of jokes, behind our backs.

In those days when I was one of the sniggerers, thin and young, I keep reminding myself that I was no less self-conscious or lacking in confidence than I am now. Only now I have something specific to blame my unease and self-consciousness on.

On the door of my office is pinned a cartoon of a lone woman addressing her fellow jurors: "He called her 'Fatso' and so she shot him! What's to deliberate?" I love that kind of chutzpa. On reflection, though, I wonder if the cartoonist is making fun of the woman justifying her own size—what we call chunky—with such an outlandish attitude.

I remember "The Girls" in the cartoons years ago. They were fat, middle-aged to older women who went out to lunch a lot, and were shown weighing themselves frequently, making excuses for what the scales reported. Only "the girls" can call themselves that these days. I wonder if we've become more sensitive than to use stereotypes to make fun of heavy older women in a cartoon. I suspect we have not changed much there or perhaps have just become more subtle.

I also remember the old "Mill and Pat" story told by a friend for years. Another friend sent him a postcard of two fat, naked women wearing only messy anklet socks, signed Mill and Pat, to embarrass him in front of their postman, his wife, and later, as it turned out, his young son who found the card hidden in his father's underwear drawer. We found this stunt hilarious, and thought the man who sent the card extremely funny and clever. Now I search for humor on the other side, like the strong woman exhorting the jury to her rage. I go to humor workshops and laugh uncontrollably when I am with my comedienne friend T. Marni Vos. Her rule is never to use humor that hurts or makes fun of others. Listening to her brings out the best in me and I can relax, knowing I will not be skewered. Drunks and hecklers and other such attendees at her club dates give her good practice in not taking advantage of other's idiosyncrasies.

But somehow I can't find what to laugh about, to make jokes about, on this side of the fat old woman divide. I have one standard anecdote I use in speeches and included in my first book, *Women and Aging: Celebrating Ourselves* (Haworth, 1992). I keep thinking another good anecdote will occur to me, but so far I have to fall back on telling this true story to illustrate that a sense of humor does relieve tension and, like guerilla warfare, strikes where we least expect it.

My husband tears jokes out of newspapers to use in his frequent speeches. I found this one beside his chair one night:

> Two women decided to streak the nursing home where they lived. As they ran past the recreation room, two old guys playing checkers looked up and one asked: "What was that?" The other responded "I don't know but whatever they had on sure needed ironing!"

When I tell this story, audiences love it and laugh hard, except there are always one or two faces frowning, in confusion or pain, doubting the humor.

I was hurt and furious and confronted my husband about his ageism and sexism. "Do you make fun of my aging skin?" I demanded. "Do women make fun of men's aging skin?" "You are just too sensitive," he responded in a traditional defense against my anger.

The next time I gave a speech, I related this episode as an example of ageism. Old friend and wise woman Amy Ebner raised her hand in the back of the room to ask, "But didn't you hear about the man who flashed the flower show at his nursing home and won first prize for best dried arrangement?" The room exploded in laughter and my story was never the same. You can imagine who did not appreciate the high humor of the second joke. Sometimes matching humor with the same is the only effective struggle to make.

I thought then that Amy Ebner's spirit would rub off on me and I'd learn how to fight back with humor. It didn't happen. I am funny, sometimes, and there are days when I giggle to myself, and nights I laugh hysterically about some current absurdity in the evening paper.

While I waited to have the oil changed in my car the other day, the serviceman showed me the very dirty air filter and suggested that I purchase a new one. I nearly laughed out loud at the image of them keeping a dirty filter at the ready to show all customers, in order to sell more air filters. Ahah, I thought, I do have a sense of humor sometimes, or at least can see something funny in ordinary interactions.

I tease my husband and respond better with each passing year to his very sharp and irreverent wit, punning, and teasing. One of my oldest friends makes himself find ten funny things a day, and when I am around him, life seems gentler. But to find the humor in being a fat old woman? How? Where?

Leafing through the current issue of *Radiance*, I see lots of smiling, assertive faces, and find a T-shirt advertised that is printed with the words, "It's not a hot flash, it's a power surge." True. Positive. Another slogan caught my eye: "A waist is a terrible thing to mind"—good take-off on Dan Quayle's remark about youngsters at risk. Another T-shirt ad declares: "If this were the 1500s, I'd be a goddess." And another is printed with: "I've just got big bones." I have a T-shirt that says "I am an outrageous old woman," which embarrasses me to wear. People always comment on how they like it; I do not know what causes my discomfort, because I *am* an outrageous old woman.

An ad in *Radiance* sent me to the telephone to order a sample copy of *Hysteria, The Women's Humor Magazine*. A review quoted, "Comics, totally loony archive photos, general silliness, feminism, and frazzle." I wonder. (Later, I found some of *Hysteria* sort of funny, a lot of it strained, even though I applaud its authors efforts; the 'zine *FAT!So?* is much more apt to make me laugh, besides feel affirmed and justifiably angry.) I receive unordered in the mail a tabloid collection of progressive cartoons and humor columns, and find the assembled humor too much, or too obvious, or too late, I do not know which, but not too funny.

I used to send my daughters copies of *Calvin and Hobbes, Cathy,* and *Sylvia* when those spoke to me, and us. *Sylvia* still does, thank heavens. We love the postcards drawn in 1940s style that say things like "I know he's a jerk! But he makes me feel so alive!!" and "Oh my god, I forgot to get married."

My Marie recently sent me from Montreal an article titled "Some Things That Make Me Puke" by Lynn Crosbie, from the August 1995 *This* Canadian magazine, in which Crosbie skewers, among other things, *Cathy* cartoons: "coy cartoons that merely perpetuate the confusion in women's lives about their genuine desires . . . about the link between anger and bingeing, and about . . . the pop-pawn of the big money women's weight loss/gain industry." Funny, angry, and true is what I found in Crosbie's courage and talent.

Ms. magazine, July/August 1996, ran a cartoon by Kaz Cooke, the Australian author of *Real Gorgeous: The Truth about Body and Beauty* (W. W. Norton & Co., 1994). Two white-coated attendants at "La Clinic Del Commerce" read their charts and tell the woman crawling toward them, "the only way for you to feel better, if we might suggest for you, Madam, a Swedish exfoliation body therapy collagen implant program, lymphatic draining tonique, total body electrolysis neo rejuvenation deep probing juices of bust firming tint remedial emergency treatment with radical eyebrow peel, lip relocation and buttocks removal regime . . . " The exhausted woman replies "I suppose a cup of tea's out of the question?" I had forgotten how much I enjoyed the drawings and cartoons in Kaz Cooke's excellent book.

No longer published, *Broomstick*, a radical magazine for and by older women, edited by Mickey Spencer and Polly Taylor from San Francisco, had a black, bawdy, ironic sense of humor, demonstrated especially in cartons called "HERdles," which were signed with the name bulbul. In going back through old copies of *Broomstick*, I realize how much I miss its radical politics and its sense of humor.

I loved the *Doonesbury* episode of a few years ago, in which lead character B.D. prepares to attend a college reunion and fantasizes about having an affair with old friend Nicole. He takes one look at her heavier body and decides against that sexual fling. Nicole catches him looking at her with shock and makes him talk about his reaction. His wife also understands his lack of enthusiasm about the reunion, smartly guessing that their old friend Nicole has gained weight. It is rare to find such accurate mainstream treatment of men's attitude toward women's weight. Three cheers for Gary Trudeau!

Rather than cartoons, however, I am looking for ways to turn criticism of my old fat self back against him or her who utters it, ways to defuse stressful situations where I feel judged on my appearance, size, and age, ways to go more gently into that good night.

As an example, I share the following: The first time my Marie was hospitalized for what turned out to be Crohn's disease—a chronic inflammation of the lower intestine of no known cause and no known cure—her doctors recommended she begin taking steroids to reduce the inflammation of her intestines. Her darling friend Bill from Montreal, visiting her at Mount Auburn Hospital in Cambridge, sat at the end of her bed, grinning, and asked: "Does this mean you'll get big muscles now, Marie?" teasing her in the midst of our terror of the disease. That kind of humor I long for, the kind that looks reality right in the face, and can still smile and tickle and come up with lightness.

There's lots of irony, plenty of sarcasm, enough satire, sufficient sardonic comments, certainly too much mocking in regard to women's appearances. Where is the real humor, that expands one's sense of self, the possibilities for joy?

Newspapers run cartoons; *Cathy* by Cathy Guisewite is forever obsessing about her size, her clothes, her attractiveness to men, albeit in a sort of humorous way, but obsessing nevertheless. I love to open *In These Times*, a bimonthly alternative newsmagazine, and look first at all its wonderful totally irreverent cartoons, led by Nicole Hollander's *Sylvia,* who says that being a writer means never having to get out of your bathrobe! I read all the cartoons first in each week's edition of *The Village Voice*, most of which are too ironic to be knee-slappers. Actually, before the cartoons, I turn immediately to Cynthia Heimel's column, "The Problem Lady" (no longer published in *The Village Voice*), where she answers with great wit, verve, and wisdom questions I suspect she sends to herself. Sometimes she just writes a plain column, sounding off on some subject on which she can no longer keep silent. All are keepers. I love the title of one of her collections of essays, "Get your tongue out of my mouth, I'm kissing you good-bye!"

I long for a light ironic attitude toward life, rather in the spirit of the T-shirt that says, "The revolution starts when the pubs close!" God forbid that I should ever make such a joke.

When people are laughing at another, they *always*, *always* say "We are laughing with you, not at you." I suspect that is not always true, but is a cover for actually laughing at someone. I know circumstances where that laughter at someone's sad tale is not cruel, but simply hilarious recognition that we've all been in the same place. Sometimes, I don't like being on the receiving end of that laughter, wanting to stamp my feet and beg others to take me seriously. That feeling comes from very long ago, from a childhood where I wished I were respected, where I felt patronized for my overly serious self. Yet even in those times when others find me funny, I can appreciate that their laughter is meant to be in solidarity, not a distancing or mocking maneuver.

Where is the humor in being fat and getting old? How can I laugh without using drugs? Not that I was a very funny drunk. Not that any are, except to each other. Where is the gentle voice that pokes fun at, all the while giving others less ammunition for criticizing and judging? How can I disarm myself and where can I learn to smile at life's foibles, and my own?

Last week in my Quaker Silent Meeting, it occurred to me that we celebrate in the face of an absurd world, under the umbrella of a world coming apart, that we must celebrate and mark both little and big joys and any passages. Such celebration helps us stay sane, stay committed to the struggle, keep healthy, and nurture our own humanness.

Even though I call myself an atheist, a secular humanist pagan atheist with Buddhist and Quaker leanings, I subscribe to *The Catholic Worker.* Many of its articles, especially the reports from the New York Maryhouse or St. Joseph House, feed my soul.

In the May 1996 *Catholic Worker*, Betty Gifford wrote an article, "A Duty of Delight," based on an outline found among her late husband Charley's writings. She tells of "the older Navajo tradition [of] a child's 'Laugh Day' . . . on which a child is seen to respond to life with unconstrained joy. . . The person who first caused the baby to laugh became a godparent . . . Laughter was thus conceived as that which brought into being the spiritual life."

She describes "laughter of naivete—the soul's purest and original response to beauty and simplicity . . . primeval laughter." The second kind of laughter, she writes, "is the laughter of paradox— one that stubbornly insists on laughing in spite of all the reasons to despair and weep. It is a courageous, almost absurd merriment— arising out of the deepest contradictions between what is now and what yet might be."

Her words, "If the first laughter is a spontaneous reply to wholeness, this second laughter reaches through the brokenness of the world to a unity not yet gained," are solace to me, reminding me that "courageous, almost absurd merriment" is something my heart longs and reaches for.

Comedienne Marni encourages people, especially those in the Elderhostels she leads, to keep a humor journal, to write down at the end of the day what struck them as funny. I wish to be struck with laughter in the midst of the day, tickled by some inner whimsy, to chuckle at some ordinary happening, be delighted and amused somewhere, somehow, at something, to be struck by the muse of humor during this not-so-funny journey.

Chapter 10

Does "Old and Fat" Mean I've Given Up?

She sat on the end of my bed in that tiny Montreal hotel room, middle daughter Marie, looking thoughtful as she searched for words to answer my question. "What do you think?" I asked her, after she had read over the rough drafts of some early chapters of this *FAT* story. As she hesitated, I thought, "Oh, my god, she thinks it's trash." Then I thought "Oh, my god, she's offended by my references to her," this 5'11", thin, graceful, beautiful daughter of mine.

What I remember of that charged moment is two things. First, Marie questioned those places where I claim that I am healthy. She did not go on to discuss my high cholesterol, but concentrated on my less than totally functional knees, how I often have trouble going up and down stairs, and how I needed to take action to repair and strengthen them.

I repeated the drill I'd been through: consultation with an orthopedic doctor, months of professional physical therapy, and final discharge. They could do no more. "As long as I can walk," I told Marie, "I think my knees are quite functional. Just because I can't squat or carry heavy loads up stairs, and sometimes have to come down stairs slowly, both feet on each step, doesn't mean I am not healthy." We concluded that part of our talk by agreeing that I needed to resume the leg-strengthening exercises I learned during the physical therapy.

So, what was her hesitation, and what did she suggest, although obliquely? That all my protestations about the culture's prejudice against fat women were defensive and that "Sometimes we need just to turn away from the culture and create our own life," this tender daughter concluded.

"What good does it do?" is often the question asked of those of us who spend our lives raging about injustice. It does me good to vent my anger by writing, even by being a voice in the wilderness, perhaps unheard and ignored, trivialized, and often scoffed at as if it were a posture to defend my indefensible size, age, or values.

Accept yourself as you are. Don't be so self-centered. Become interested in helping others. Quit the obsession with what you look like. All these are familiar exhortations in these days flavored with the New Age "you are what you think" philosophy.

Such adages may be true and appropriately apply to me, to my rage, to my dust-mop self going through the world looking under beds, collecting every piece of injustice, each unfairness voiced or manifested toward women—especially women heavy and/or old—children, poor people, minorities, the dispossessed, and the marginalized everywhere.

I may be screaming about the loss of my youth and "attractiveness" and blaming it on the culture. I may be hiding my head in the sand when I refuse to weigh myself or be weighed, not wanting to see the numbers that would shame me into "doing something about it," not wanting to be defined each day by numbers on a scale.

My medical doctor said, upon first reading my high cholesterol numbers, that losing 15 pounds would automatically reduce those findings. When a stress test three years ago showed "some" artery blockage, which vanished by the end of the test, my doctor suggested that I increase my exercise, which I did from 30 minutes to 45 every day. Rain or shine, tired or not, I now walk, swim, or ride my exercise bicycle 45 minutes a day.

The lovely English professor who was discussing his diet at that Nebraskans for Peace potluck later came dangerously close to a major heart attack. He has lost 55 pounds in a hospital heart attack recovery program, and tells me he thinks about food all the time. He looks gaunt compared to his former fat self.

A friend who also has high cholesterol takes medication to control it. He continued to eat candy daily, not exercise, and figured the pills would be enough to keep his cholesterol from rising. His cholesterol rose anyway; now he's lost some weight and several inches around his waist. The pills my doctor's assistant prescribed sat untouched in my bathroom cabinet, until I finally gave up that $45 worth of medicine and flushed them down the toilet. Their side effects, the worst of which is to think I can give up exercise and eat unwisely if I take them, encourage me not to use them.

So why don't I just shut up, lose some weight, and quit complaining that the world no longer considers me attractive? Why don't I do as a couple I know, both medical doctors and shirttail relatives, did a few years ago—go completely off fat, lose some weight, and get their cholesterol down to medically approved levels? Am I too lazy, too undisciplined?

These are the questions daughter Marie triggered in me, perhaps not questions she asked, but certainly ones I must face.

She also gently indicated, at least I thought so, that I might have "given up," calling myself a fat old woman a self-fulfilling prophecy. Have I?

Her words were, "The whole thing is kind of a paradox; denial does nothing. You might as well face reality. On the other hand, there is the whole self-fulfilling prophecy thing. We are kind of talking about definitions here. So old is accurate, true. But you know the person who concentrates on the world so much that she stays forever young."

"What do you mean by that?" I ask her. "Oh, you know, the 70 or 80-year-old with a glint in her eye, a childlike quality. Something about them is renewed, fresh, always open, growing, learning. So it's a paradox."

Yes, as much as I rail against our misuse of the word "old," it is in fact badly used by almost everyone I know. It is a synonym for tired, lonely, forgetful, boring, inactive, sexless, uninteresting, complaining, crabby, bent-over, slow, despondent, messy. Just exactly as "fat" means sloppy, overeater, lack of exercise, funny, undisciplined, ugly, embarrassing, out of control, messy. Marie's words to describe the "forever young" old person are words we reserve only for the young, and are certainly never descriptions of old people, even though we are describing an old person. But I know what she means.

These cultural definitions of old and fat are reflections of the cultural rules that women must be thin in order to be valued and old women must be caretakers to be appreciated, unless they are Joan Collins look-alikes.

In an op-ed piece in the May 15, 1996 *Lincoln Journal Star*, I wrote the following:

> Since old constitutes one-third of our lives, whoever decided that women in particular are to pretend it does not exist, that we can "transcend it"?
>
> Our cultural definition of the word old is wrong but fierce, our view of what constitutes old, narrow and cruel. . . At what cost do we miss the journey of old age, that surprising, profound, bewildering, rich time of becoming something we've never been before? Jungian Helen Luke warns people to face the journey into old age, letting go of the ego-driving satisfactions of one's younger days.
>
> What about the rest of us [besides rich and famous thin old women], being told that becoming old is a myth, and that if we just try hard enough we can look young and be successful in the world's terms? We need something more real, something more true, something more creative than insistence that we keep on doing what we're doing, which requires surgery on one's body and/or constant satisfaction of an ambitious ego.

Another paradox is that when I use accurate words to describe myself, I indeed am looked upon as someone who is no longer attractive or useful, and am giving in to exactly what the culture describes as old and fat. Maggie Kuhn, who founded the Gray Panthers at age 65, exhorted us to do something outrageous every day. Calling one's self old and fat undoubtedly qualifies.

Old friend Joyce used to tell me I "dressed down." Her style is gorgeous African, her head in lovely dreadlocks, her jewelry exqui-site and always perfect for her outfits. While we lived in the same town, she switched over to wearing only Birkenstocks, and I did too. I know I'd look less dumpy wearing stylish, even low-heeled pumps with dress-up outfits, but I don't want to go back, and neither do my feet.

My three daughters and I have long had discussions about female adornment—jewelry, make-up, clothing, perfume. They worry that I am throwing the baby out with the bathwater in my anger at my culture's rules for women's acceptability. Marie also worries, I think, that I am angry at all men, and not just, as I assure her, at patriarchal systems. I might just need to reread carefully a favorite book, *Breaking all the Rules: Feeling Good and Looking Great No Matter What Your Size* by Nancy Roberts (Penguin Books, 1986) in order to concentrate on "feeling good and looking great" instead of taking on the world.

In the first months of this year, I have taken several steps, all alternative, that I consider helpful to my health and to lowering my cholesterol. I rehearse them in my mind, as if naming them justifies my not dieting or going on a total no-fat regime. I took a fifth step with a trusted friend, that part of a 12-step program that consists of writing down all my resentments and reading them to another person. Her wise and gentle suggestions allowed my judging self to let go of most of them. I connect the bile stored in my gall bladder, with the bile of resentment. I have done a gall bladder cleansing, with apple juice and olive oil. A friend performed a Reike treatment on my body, concentrating on my gall bladder. I continue to be rigorously faithful to that 45 minutes of daily exercise, take several food supplements that reduce cholesterol, such as fish oil, garlic, and bromelain, and intend to start lifting weights, strongly suggested for reducing cholesterol.

In the next year, my cholesterol came down to acceptable levels, and I had to have my gall bladder removed. I was embarrassed to have such a middle-class health problem; my doctor assured me it was from a lifetime of a "western hemisphere diet." The tiny pocket of reserve bile used to digest fat was filled with stones and I never knew when one of its wildly painful attacks would hit me, driving myself to a hospital emergency room during the last one, an extremely dangerous driver in that altered state from the wrenching pain.

A thoughtful response to "Fat Is Your Problem" by Nomy Lamm in the March/April 1996 *Ms.* magazine came from someone describing himself as a "fat white guy." Michael Stasko of Columbus, Ohio, writes,

> I need to be concerned about my health. I don't want to lose weight because of what the assholes in society think of fat people . . . but if I don't find a way to change my health now, then my illnesses will happen [hereditary high blood pressure, diabetes, and heart failure] sooner rather than later.

Lamm, who is from Olympia, Washington, is the creator of the 'zine *i'm so fucking beautiful.* A young woman dancer/performer, she writes a passionate, blunt, eloquent and lucid, radical "guest room" article from the point of view of a fat person, member of "The Fat Grrrl Revolution," and laments, "Sometimes I am afraid to perform because I don't want to deal with fat oppression . . . it's really important to me that I be taken seriously [as an artist]" (*Ms.,* March/April, 1996).

Now having read Nomy's first three 'zines, which are wild, radical, brutally honest, diverse, and thoughtful, I am excited and enlightened through her ability to research and write about the deep issues of fat oppression within a political-economic framework (i.e., fat-hating is not just a personal choice). Capitalism *needs* people to hate fat in order to sustain itself. Without fat-hate the $33 billion a year diet industry would collapse. Despite substantial medical evidence that fat is not caused by overeating and that only 1 to 10% of all fat people who go on reducing diets will be capable of keeping off the weight, we are still told to 'keep on trying.'"

Nony describes the emotional work she does in *isfb* 'zine number three: "I need to make myself talk about this or I'll forget what I'm trying to do, get too caught up in daily life, self-hatred, numbness." She writes, perceptively, about appearance: "It is a gross oversimplification of fat liberation to say it's just about 'not judging on appearances' . . . for one thing fat oppression isn't just about 'appearances' . . . those of us who do have sight rely on that sense to tell us a lot about the world and . . . what I choose to do with my body and my appearance says a lot about me and I think that this line of thinking of ignoring people's appearances is a total cop-out."

She lists "a quick list of rules for you to keep in mind" in 'zine number two:

1. fat is not ugly
2. fat people do not lack control
3. fat people do not need to lose weight
4. we do not make 'fat jokes'
5. fat is punk rock
6. you do not call yourself 'fat' if you're not. learn the difference.

7. diets are 20 times more unhealthy than being fat
8. i am not ashamed of my body
9. i am susceptible to pain. don't try to hurt me.
10. if you consider me a threat, if you fear me now, then just wait. the fat grrrl revolution has begun."

My Marie may be right, that I am tilting at ineradicable windmills, and that I am not doing what I should to be truly healthy mentally, emotionally, and physically. Overworked as his quote is, I cannot help but think of Rainer Maria Rilke's words: "Be patient toward all that is unsolved in your heart and try to love the questions themselves."

I may be self-justifying, but I am also following the passionate urgings within myself to rail against the pain and injustice caused in this world by defining women by what they look like, by judging others by a narrow, ridiculous, random, irrational standard of what is attractive, by trying to arrange a world that shows only what our eyes have been trained to like and approve of.

The long road for me is obviously to love this old, heavy body, to clothe it happily and comfortably, and, as we say, "get on with it," not leaving anything out of the living of this strange awkward journey. I accept no paeans to my beautiful spirit, as a way of ignoring my body or making up for its failings. My spirit may be beautiful, but I live in this physical body and need to discover what it has to teach me in this lifetime, especially, I hope, gratitude for its longevity and power—and beauty.

Chapter 11

This Body I Live In

In looking for all my May Sarton books, especially *Journal of a Solitude*, which I cannot find, and going through a disorganized collection of articles, books, and magazines about weight and size prejudice, *and* pawing through a drawer of bills to find insurance forms, *and* trying to get enough loose ends tied up so that I could get to today's writing assignment—"This Body I Live in" chapter—I flipped open *Chop Wood, Carry Water*, the 1984 classic "guide to finding spiritual fulfillment in Everyday Life" (Jeremy P. Tarcher, 1984).

The "Tuning the Body" chapter opens with the Indian or Tibetan story of an old blind turtle who lives in the depths of the ocean and swims to the top of the sea every thousand years. "Imagine that there is a wooden ring floating somewhere on the surface of the ocean, and think of how rare it would be for the blind turtle, coming up for air once every thousand years, to put its head through the wooden ring. It is just that rare, say the Tibetans, for a being to gain human birth" (p. 159).

My breath sucked in, in surprise and delight. "To the Tibetans, to be born with a 'precious human body' is to be born with the perfect vehicle for obtaining realization or enlightenment. . . . The human body is considered a temple, the reflection or embodiment of the cosmos, the form of divinity."

I remember that thought last, that the body is a temple of God, from my Christian days. What captured my attention, though, was the idea that *this body I live in* is the vehicle, the perfect vehicle for the realization of the life into which I was born.

What probably rules me more, however, is that Christian Science upbringing that, as I remember it, insisted that the body is unreal, only mind is real, that "sin, sickness, disease, and death" are unreal. That famous body/mind split in the West, embodied in Mary Baker Eddy's teachings, was an integral part of my upbringing.

In addition to Christian Science, my sisters and I learned from our just-barely-out-of-Victorian-times mother only to look in a mirror long enough to comb our hair or put on a dab of pastel lipstick; never to glance at reflections of ourselves in store windows; and to consider all body functions as gross, except eating when done with proper manners, all other needs to be taken care of out of sight, quickly and without comment.

Bathroom doors in our house were kept almost closed when no one was in there. Imagine a guest actually seeing a toilet from a hall or other room! When we smelled a skunk on the road, as our mother drove us to Camp Fire Camp in the Black Hills, she recommended we "rise above it" instead of, as we were wont to do, collapsing in laughter and yelling "Phew!" or "That stinks!"—the word "stink" we were not permitted to use within our parents' hearing. We called body parts by their "polite" names: stomach, not belly; rear or back end, not buttocks; bosom, not breasts (the word "boobs" had not yet reached our area or had not yet been invented); and there were no words in our vocabulary for male or female genitals, maybe just "down there" if anything. "Going to the bathroom" was "going to the bathroom" (see, I still can't say anything else in public), not to piss or pee, or to take a dump or shit. Our naughty cousins "farted" but we did not say the word nor mention such an act. Menstruation was, of course, "the curse," and we learned as if in our genes to avoid wearing white clothing on those days.

My bawdy self appeared uninvited one day, from which unconscious surfacing I suffered extreme embarrassment for quite a number of years afterwards. Sitting on our lawn with my sister Ann's boyfriend, while she was inside tending to her nosebleed, I said, "Now she's bleeding from both ends." Her boyfriend was shocked; he told Ann, who told my mother, who confronted me with deep shame for saying such a thing. In that era, one rarely talked about menstruation, except briefly with a girlfriend or mother, and certainly never in front of boys or men.

While I'm remembering body embarrassments, once at the public swimming pool, in junior-high years (that "House of Pain") in my two-piece suit that covered me thoroughly, since bikinis were decades away, I sat on steps leading up to the diving board. Unknown to me, the elastic on the one leg of my suit had come loose, exposing me from below, where the boys could see my pubic hair and perhaps catch a dim look at my "bottom." Shame was the issue then; the event was not just a matter-of-fact moment about a loose bathing suit or inadvertent minor embarrassment.

In junior high, our gang used to pile into one of the boy's father's cars (girls were not permitted to drive family cars as early as the boys were), drive out to the foot of the Bluffs, and spend the evening regaling one another with dirty jokes—stupid dirty jokes, I might add. I went home and told my parents a joke I'd heard one ribald evening, not having a clue what it meant: Did you hear the one about the guy who visited his girl friend and pole-vaulted over the house? Big erection was the point. I realized I'd done something wrong, but did not get the full message of terrible shame until the next day when my mother told me how shocked my father was, how embarrassed he was, and how disappointed he was in me.

I didn't even know what it meant. But I knew I was a bad person for repeating the joke, and that any allusion to an erection, about which I knew nothing, was beyond the pale.

Leafing through various books also reminded me of the body therapies I have done in this adult, alternative-to-my-family life. For years, I have been fortunate enough to have a weekly hour-long massage; years ago I went through a series of Rolfing sessions, a deep connective tissue release, which I loved; today, I do sun salutes, yoga postures that stretch the entire body, when I get up in the morning; yoga classes used to be part of my weekly schedule; I have taken three series of Tai Chi classes, eventually giving up practice and forgetting the movements; for some years, I regularly took classes and had appointments for the incredibly gifted body work of a Feldenkrais method practitioner (a sequence of precise movements to increase awareness, coordination, and flexibility, and to provide new learning opportunities to the neural-muscular system); an out-of-the-mainstream chiropractor has been a good friend for years, monthly appointments for his gentle adjustments and pioneering techniques part of my health routine; I also used to do "breath work" with my regular therapist, to retrieve old pain in order to heal it.

I have never been able to fast with any success, on infrequent attempts getting to four o'clock in the afternoon and deciding that I must eat. For several months, I underwent colonic cleansing at another chiropractor's office, the results of which I knew to be beneficial but which I barely endured. The process reminds me entirely too much of enemas; and particularly since gall bladder surgery in 1995, my body functions extremely well in that regard.

A long talk with a friend yesterday had us reviewing with each other those places where we feel good about our bodies. I contributed only the women's night at a spa in Denver, which I attended with my youngest daughter years ago: the sight and comfort of women of all ages, sizes, and shapes, naked, showering, sitting in the steam room, in the sauna, in the whirlpool, awaiting massage, immediately chased my body self-consciousness away and let me revel in myself and other women for the evening. I also contributed the memory of the "coed" hot-tubbing we used to do on our Wednesday afternoons off during intensive values clarification/realization week-long training seminars.

I also remember with some discomfort that we who were thin or "normal" sized were chastised by our sensitive leader Sid Simon, not to insist everyone go naked into the hot tubs. It had come to his attention that the large and heavy women who were part of the hot-tubbing gang on Wednesday afternoons, felt the need to cover up their bodies with swim suits, feeling discriminated against in the group enthusiasm to be "free" and naked together.

In *Chop Wood, Carry Water*, "Tuning the Body" concludes with Paul Winter, a musician who specializes in earth music and ecology, listing his daily tools for reconnecting: sun, song, sax, stretch, sprint, stough, smile. Sun equals outdoors in any weather; Song is singing, chanting, humming; Sax is, of course, his horn, which he plays for five minutes every morning; Stretch is yoga; Sprint is running, jogging; Stough is a series of breathing exercises taught by Carl Stough, with whom Winter studies; and Smile is to produce a chemical change in one's being.

Every day. Ah . . . I long to get back to meditation; do more yoga than I do; I exercise 45 minutes a day—walking, swimming, or indoor biking seven days a week; smile without meaning to; and go outdoors every day. Intentional breathing, humming, and playing an instrument (like all good middle-class children, I took piano lessons growing up) have no regular place in my day, except for those times I breath deeply to calm down or resist anxiety. (After writing in my journal first thing in the morning, and reading some daily meditation books, I do Hugh Prather's suggestion of a few breaths: inhale to "My mind is clear" and exhale to "My body is still"). Perhaps I need to design or at least recognize other reconnection and centering behaviors and rituals, especially of my own. Writing is a great one for me, as is half an hour alone, reading my store of progressive magazines.

I know, and sometimes remember to do, lots of New Age body exercises, such as asking my cramping stomach what it wants; holding my childhood doll Marie close to my body and thereby knowing what is going on in me (which comes as if it were Marie's feelings); and screwing up my courage to spend a few minutes looking at my naked self in a mirror (where I see on my wiggly self a long appendix scar where the 1940s doctor told mother "I checked her bedroom furniture while I was in there," such sexism not lost on me later; a stomach stretched from three pregnancies, weight gain, and weight loss; a long scar on my backside from a toboggan accident where a tree branch went in my buttock and out below my waist without hitting any organs; four tiny scars from gall bladder laser surgery, one where they pull that organ out through the belly button; breasts now large and droopy, a change from that flat-chested early adolescence; short, strong legs; strong, upright shoulders; a fatty tumor under my chin, making me look more double-chinned than I am [which could be reduced with liposuction]; mottled, untanned skin after years of sunbathing to be fashionably tan; a head of short, silvery hair; wrinkled face; and faded blue eyes). I often reread several pamphlets of "Energy Tune-Ups" advice and occasionally actually do one or two of them, such as the Chinese Do-In exercises. My body carries on its own health regime, without my direction, when it yawns, wiggles, stretches, shivers, scrunches, and blinks.

Once I heard about a kind of dance therapy, which sounds great— someday! As youngsters, we loved to dance, which I haven't done for forty-some years. For years, I have felt drawn to clowning, as if painting on another face and wearing crazy clothing would allow me to become some of who I am inside: shy, awkward, silly, sad, unproductive.

Petting my beloved cat, rescued from Animal Control after all the girls' childhood feline companions died, two after especially long lives, is surely part of a ritual of health, of connection. His demand for attention and my need to feel his soft purring fur is one small way I am reconnecting with touch, feeling, and mindfulness on this journey to live in my body.

SECTION II:
WHAT THE OUTSIDE
WORLD BELIEVES

Chapter 12

I Am Not Your Punching Bag!

I feel like a punching bag today. I consider that I may be a piece of litmus paper going through the world, tiny feelers out for any mention of my disease of discomfort with my size.

Reading Erica Jong's *Fear of Fifty, A Midlife Memoir* (Harper-Collins, 1994), I sailed along happily, albeit sojourning in the land foreign to me of rich, intellectual, New York Russian Jews, until I stumbled across this description of the adult daughter of an old friend of Jong's grandparents: "In those days, she was pudgy, with close-cropped pepper and salt hair and the flowing clothes fatties used to wear to disguise themselves from themselves" (p. 135).

FATTIES, I screamed inside. Is that who we are, the *FATTIES*? Am I only disguising myself from myself? What do we *FATTIES* wear now?

Erica Jong prides herself, perhaps rightly so, on her acceptance of all colors and sexual preferences in her friends and lovers. Throughout *Fear of Fifty*, however, I caught hints of her need to stay thin, beautiful, and sexually attractive. There is never a sentence, a phrase, a word, however, that suggests she considers herself anything else but. Wherever she went, married or single, beautiful, interesting men flocked to her, according to the memoir. She never says "flocked." That is my anger at her coming out sideways. But she never lacked for willing partners, most of whom sought her out. She faces insecurity in other areas of her life, but I do not perceive any about her ability to attract men.

Then ("then" I say with high dudgeon and serious sighs of being put upon) I opened my Tuesday, May 30, 1995, *Omaha World-Herald* to read the occasional column by a lovely woman my husband and I admire. From the "Wellness Letter" from the University of

California at Berkeley, this writer and activist quotes "how best to combat increasing girth," in an article titled "Weight, Fat, Set Point, Counterpoint."

Arguing from the point that "many Americans are overweight and more entered the category in the last decade," the article she refers to "stated firmly that obesity has a lot more to do with how much we eat and how little we exercise." (Couch potatoes have never been my target audience. I speak for people who veer from the norm, women who are not size 6, 8 or 10, some attractive, some perhaps not in your eyes, some who exercise and some who don't.)

Attacking a Rockefeller University "study on body weight, which concluded that obese people have a resistance to maintaining weight loss—that is, their own metabolism defeats them," the Berkeley newsletter discounts the "set point" theory that "is part of the jargon of many diet books."

The newsletter states, "What researchers do not say . . . is that 'metabolic resistance' does not go on forever. Eventually, the body adjusts to the new weight. Metabolic adjustments that occur when you lose or gain weight are complex and usually not only temporary but small."

My friend concludes, "The problem with blaming 'set points' or 'obesity genes' or anything else as the inability to shed pounds, is that it is such a convenient cop-out. People who read these studies believe them and just give up." She paraphrases the wellness report: "Increasing obesity is more easily explained by the availability of gasoline and fast food than by genetics or the set-point theory."

Nowhere in the newspaper column or wellness newsletter do we see a definition of obesity; nowhere do we read the clearly implied assumption that thin is healthier than fat; nowhere do we read this older woman's also implicit assumption that we are to believe she is talking only about health, and not about her appearance. The writer concludes with "a whole new regime" to cut down on the number of nonfat cookies she eats, to put "intensity" into her exercises, and to lift weights. She writes, "It's a great feeling to take charge of your own health, to get moving, to feel healthy things happening to your body."

Exhortations to do better, to be nicer, to shape up, to work hard to match what the culture suggests is our destiny, make me angry, especially the ones loaded with patronizing observations of people who do not "shape up." Does anyone not notice the dissonance? At a meeting years ago, I listened to a tiny, slim, stylish woman speak about how she was going to lose 10 pounds and work on accepting herself more. I find those goals mutually exclusive.

Ex-cuuse me! She had also seen the movie *Pretty Woman* over the weekend and couldn't figure out why she was depressed. Here she was, long divorced, with a good job, certainly fitting the world's definition of attractive woman. Did she want to be rescued by a hunk, established in his apartment, to have sex with him on demand, filling those hours between his appearances by staying pretty and available? Dear goddesses!

I am entirely suspicious of advertisements, such as one that trumpets "All About Women and Healthy Eating"—this one sponsored by the University of Nebraska Medical Center and the Olson Center for Women's Health. (Is there a center for Men's Health? Does the Olson center pay any attention to the fact that it is primarily women who contract eating disorders?) The come-on statistic, running in reverse block down the side of the large advertisement, reports, "Up to 25 percent of college females may suffer from either anorexia nervosa or bulimia nervosa." With the caveat "American girls and women are bombarded by images and misinformation about how their bodies should look and the measure they should take to achieve the 'perfect' body. . . the right information about variety, balance and moderation is lost. . . . take the mystery out of eating right, help women and girls understand healthy weight management practices and help them recognize the early signs of disordered eating and exercise."

Let's see: how many calories does "eating right" imply—how many meals a day, how many grams of fat, how much protein, how much sugar? Does "balance and moderation" mean somewhere between size 8 and 12? What does the Olson Center for Women's Health advise as "healthy weight management?" The subjects listed by the two experts for this program are "Healthy and Normal Eating," by a clinical nutritionist, and "When Healthy Eating Becomes Disordered" from a psychologist. Is normal eating anything that does not make a woman fat? Or is it truly the diabetic who gives up processed sugar, or the person with high cholesterol who watches her consumption of fat? Is "disordered" eating to be determined by what we weigh and what another thinks of what we look like? I overreact, I know. I simply fear all women get skewered in ads that may only concern anorexia and bulimia.

Even in a somewhat tender story (in a *New York Times* article carried by the July 25, 1996 *Omaha World-Herald*) about female bonding at salons and spas, where women get refreshed from hair roots to toenails, writer Lisa W. Foderaro describes Thea Winarsky, a 29-year-old lawyer, at a salon for manicure and pedicure, who laments, "It's an added stress when you're busy working to have to come and do this, but you do. You really have to look polished and finished; otherwise people at work will wonder if *THERE'S SOME-THING NOT QUITE UNDER CONTROL IN YOUR LIFE*" [emphasis mine]. How clear it is that the issue is control, and for women who generally don't share power in this country, control over one's body and one's appearance is the scrap blown up to career-damaging proportions.

The *Bottom Line*, a splendid publication about "Getting the most for your time and money," in its June 15, 1995 issue features in its Self-Improvement section "Proven Strategies for Losing Weight" by Stephen P. Gullo, PhD, of the Institute for Health and Weight Sciences. That institute "offers one-on-one coaching to retrain eating habits and attitudes toward food." Gullo is the author of—are you ready for this—*Thin Tastes Better: Control Your Food Triggers and Lose Weight Without Feeling Deprived.*

Under learning to "abandon your deprivation mentality," Gullo recommends, "Knowing how to say, *no, thank you* to food is saying *yes* to a healthier, thinner body." Of course, thinner is *HEALTHIER.* This president of the Institute for Health and Weight Sciences (I am sure Gullo or his marketing company worked hard to come up with this ambiguous, scientific-sounding title) is, judging by his interview comments and the title of his book, interested in helping people lose weight under the guise of *HEALTH.* Some of his eating suggestions surely apply to establishing healthier eating patterns, such as figuring out your own eating patterns and which ones you want to change. " . . . [Y]ou have to be especially careful about snacking while you're watching TV or overeating when you're tired." (Brilliant). Nowhere does he suggest listening to one's body, he only talks about conquering it.

Apples and oranges, no pun intended, get cleverly, subtly mixed, as in this advice about "changing your food talk": "Seldom do we say," reports Gullo, *"Is it so good that I'm willing to wear a larger size for it?* or *Do I really want to worsen my cholesterol level by eating that?"* In the "abandon your deprivation mentality" section, Gullo talks about being "a prisoner of a body that has become overweight and sick from poor eating habits." Notice how over-weight and sick are paired, as larger size and cholesterol are in the first example.

A big headline in the morning newspaper reports, "Obesity traced to gene defect that interferes with feedback" (*Lincoln Star*, June 1, 1995). The story talks about "A genetic defect that causes the brain to read 'stop eating' messages from the stomach as 'eat more' [which] may be the primary cause of obesity, scientists reported Thursday."

Oh, god, here we go again—the *FATTIES* eat too much. The Cox News Service article quotes a study by Dr. Jose F. Caro, former chairman of medicine at Thomas Jefferson University in Philadelphia and current Vice President of Endocrine Research at Eli Lilly Laboratories in Indianapolis. His study, published in the *Journal of Clinical Investigation*, was based on tissue samples from 16 healthy adults, half of whom were lean, half obese.

> In lean humans, the obesity gene appears to cause fat cells to secrete a satiety factor (appetite suppressant) that tells the brain how much fat storage is left . . . If fat storage increases, the obesity gene sends a message to the cell to produce more protein. If fat storage decreases, the satiety factor decreases and the brain activates appetite to avoid malnutrition. In this way, feeding is regulated to keep normal weight. But when this delicate feedback loop system fails, the brain never learns that fat storage is ample, which results in continued food cravings.

Caro said it should be possible to produce a drug within a few years to make the gene behave normally and shut down any unnatural (*UNNATURAL!*) urge to eat in people who are now affected. Some 75 million Americans are considered obese.

"Even if a 'magic pill' is discovered, these other environmental factors will have to be considered," said Caro, who described his findings as a 'breakthrough' in the *WAR ON FAT.*

There it is, the *WAR ON FAT.* I hope the good doctor makes his fortune on that "magic pill." Surely he will. Haven't we all been looking for the "magic pill" to make us the perfect shape and size, to keep us from becoming addicts of any sort, to keep unease, anxiety, and depression out of our lives? Could we all just zone out on tranquilizers in this brave new world?

It is common knowledge that it takes 20 minutes for the brain to receive the message that the stomach is full, thus one should eat slowly and deliberately, and stop when one feels full, giving the brain time to get the signal. We could call it a "delicate feedback loop system" if we want to.

There are many in-depth studies that disprove the notion that large, fat, heavy—whatever you want to call them—people eat more than thin people. There are also many large, fat, heavy people who exercise regularly, wear stylish clothing, have good jobs, healthy friendships, travel widely, and generally live productive, rational, happy lives.

So there. How I wish to stop reacting like a geiger counter or a seismograph or my litmus paper self to the current *WAR AGAINST ANYONE WHO IS DIFFERENT FROM WHAT SOMEONE ELSE SAYS IS PROPER!* Standing our ground is hard these days and it looks like it's getting harder.

Chapter 13

Is Ugly True?

I lay on the table face up, glowing from a nice massage at this vacation resort in Nice, France, which is the site of a convention for my husband. The tiny masseuse touched my shoulders and upper chest and said, "This part of your body is nice, but," and her hand lightly touched my stomach, "this is not."

If I had not been lying down, I would have fallen over in a faint at this surprise attack, this rudeness, this impolitic remark from someone in business to make people feel better. This undisguised attempt was, I assume, to sell me face cream for my wrinkles, lotion for the brown spots on my hands and temples, and an exercise regime for my "not nice" protruding belly.

God almighty, do I deserve this? At that ridiculous moment, I thanked her for her concern, got dressed, paid, even tipped her so as not to be further shamed, and left, trying hard not to give in to feeling defeated, embarrassed, socked in the stomach as it were, and resigned to being ugly.

At home in the United States, it's bad enough to be large and old, but in France, site of the massage ruined by that last remark, it is worse. Appearance, at least in the large cities we visited (Paris and Nice) appeared to be a big issue for women; I saw small, thin, well-dressed women everywhere, shoring up the stereotypical notion these days that the lazy indulgent Americans are especially fat.

We didn't see what in the old days would have been called peasants—big-boned, strong farm workers pictured so idyllically in large canvasses by European artists. Even in these United States, size is a class issue (also gender, sexual orientation, and ethnic), middle and upper-class women spending lots more time and money on dieting and on procedures to stay young and thin. For people closer to the earth, or perhaps less influenced by the sophistication or fashion trends of big cities and enclaves of the rich and well-to-do, one's size is simply one's size, one's age a matter of fact, not something to be hated, criticized, or tampered with endlessly.

But on that trip, fraught with dreadful low self-esteem brought on by comparison with the other people we were with, with my husband's positive comments about other women's clothing, how nice they looked, and none for me, I fell, only noticing consciously that something was wrong, into that old female pit of thinking I was unattractive, unless someone told me differently, and therefore only to be tolerated, endured, and patronized.

Any sane person will respond immediately that such a mood could not have been produced by any outside agent, that I was and am responsible for extricating myself from such a morass, facing the leftover blaming and resentments later from more solid ground. I agree, but I didn't know what had happened, what I had let happen, and suffered off and on for days.

One night when our group went out together, I remember well that my husband's face lit up at my appearance—a red silk blouse over a bright skirt. Even though red is his favorite color and he is always comments positively when I wear something red, I figured that his reaction indicated only that this outfit covered up my fat more than usual. I reveled in this approval, relaxing and being more outgoing with our traveling group.

It has taken me this many words to get to the "truth" I am trying to deny, that appearance standards in this world are based on reality, that there *is* ugly and pretty, and that I am an idiot to think otherwise.

I preach against "in the eye of the beholder," feeling strongly that we need to widen our appreciation, not just to tolerate whatever is not fashionably beautiful. Looking past appearances to a beautiful soul may have its benefits, but why not consider the exterior beautiful, too?

Lucy Grealy, author of *Autobiography of a Face* (Houghton-Mifflin, 1994), which is a story about being disfigured by cancer of the jaw, writes in the May/June 1996 *Ms.* "guest room" column, "Epilogue of a Face," which is about being on a media tour for her book.

Gradually she realized,

> My book, and my life, were being made into a cliche. While
> many people did "get" my book and understood that it wasn't
> so much about disfigurement as about self—how we define
> ourselves, how we seek things and people in the world to tell
> us who we are—others definitely did not. . . . Particularly in
> the fashion magazines, my story was suddenly all about how
> "beauty is really on the inside . . . it doesn't matter what you look
> like . . . and society puts too much emphasis on looks." (p. 96)

Insisting on NOT blaming the fashion industry for too much
emphasis on looks . . . "that's their job. I am not here to tell people to
stop wanting to be beautiful," Grealy came to realize

> that the aesthetic of the cliches they wanted from me under-
> scored the very kinds of prejudices I'd had to reject in the first
> place, simply in order to survive my original ordeal with can-
> cer and its aftermath.
>   It's not the idea that "beauty only truly comes from within"
> that I objected to—although I reject being the poster child for
> inner beauty—it was the platitudinous way the interviewers
> wanted me to say it . . . The danger of the "neat package,"
> whether it's skin cream or catchy sayings, is that it doesn't allow
> for our complicated, often conflicting responses toward things.
> Somewhere along the line we become convinced that the goal
> is to have only clear and harmonious feelings about things. This
> is the idea from which both the most innocuous commercial
> slogans and the most dangerous political propaganda are born.

Calling on old friends a few years ago, we were pleased that their
grown daughter stopped by and that we got to see her. When we left,
I remarked to my husband, "Isn't she (the daughter) a lovely young
woman?" He looked at me quizzically and did not respond. He kept
looking at me as if trying to figure out whatever I meant.

This young woman is extraordinarily skilled in social interaction;
she is pretty, funny, friendly, competent, well-employed, independent, thoughtful, and large. I could list more descriptions of how I
reacted to her delightful presence. I would guess that my husband

was "concerned" about her weight and supposed that to be the reason she was not married. I can only guess because he said nothing, continuing for a few minutes to look puzzled at my reaction.

I liked what she looked like. I could not separate this charming young woman from her body—that was part of her, too, and I liked all of her. Would I have had the same reaction had she been shy? I can answer an emphatic "yes" to that. If she'd been rude, too busy to talk to old friends of her parents, too self-concerned to be nice to her mom and dad, or angry at herself for being large, I might not have been able to see through that to her very real beauty.

Junior-high boys make terrible comments about girls, so insecure themselves that they project onto young women epithets such as "dog," "pig," and "hog." In checking with a mother of an early teenage boy and girl, I heard more than I bargained for. "I am so glad neither of my children is going into junior high overweight," she candidly reported. "They are merciless and brutal [about fat]." "They seem to think large is okay but they put down fat girls like they do about a girl with loose morals" ("slut" apparently one of the descriptions of a fat girl). "They also refer to body parts, such as 'big butt' and 'you could surf on it.'"

"Overweight" is a word we all use, and we know what it means. How can I fight that, demanding that people explain and justify calling someone "overweight," insisting myself on using "weighs more than average" as an accurate substitute. Who decides what is "overweight" and what is "underweight?" Those wretched old insurance company height and weight charts, even the revised ones? To what standard do we give allegiance when we say "overweight?" Any size that would cause a junior-high boy to make fun of it?

So there is "ugly" out there. There are "dogs" and "old hags" and "crows" and "witches" and people whose size causes others to be embarrassed and to barely tolerate them. There are ugly women and beautiful women, and fat women with "such a beautiful face" and classy dressers of any size or shape.

We don't have time for or interest in the ugly ones, the fat ones, the old ones, even the "unattractive" ones. We surround ourselves with images of starving women, bottom ribs removed, anorexic, bulimic, skeleton-like, reminiscent of extreme starvation, protruding pelvic bones, gaunt—gorgeous we think. We buy clothing a size too small and vow that we'll "diet down to it." We sign up for programs that advertise "weight management" to hide the truth that they are just another diet, another way for a hospital or other organization to make money.

We feel sorry for the ugly ones, the pathetic old ones, the sloppy fat ones, the women too large to be some man's "little woman." We patronize anyone who doesn't meet our standards by repeating in various forms that old junior-high line, said while smirking, "But she has a great personality." We all know of many instances of friends and acquaintances whose husbands tell them, "I'll divorce you if you get fat." Junior-high thinking is given the substance of adult truth by our behavior. We demean and diminish, ignore, and tolerate those whose appearance does not bring us pleasure, profoundly conditioned as we are by our culture's deadly and false standards.

My eye looked up for a moment, needing to pause and figure out where to go with this attempt to face and therefore disarm the prevailing opinion that would keep me victim and prisoner. Taped to the top frame of my computer monitor I saw this, from *Framing History* by Virginia Carmichael (University of Minnesota Press, 1993): "The greatest threat to effective work for positive change will inhere in the degree to which an identification of the opposition allows us, through splitting and projection to remain voluntarily blind to our own daily dependency on the order we would change" (p. 222).

Oh, god, yes, is that true!

I am not blind, nor do I consider that I must see beyond physical appearances or see with eyes of love in order to ignore those appearances. But what I am partially blind to is my "own daily dependency"—heaven help me—on the order I would change.

How can I demand of the world around me that which it cannot give? My daughter Mary demanded of me, during a low point in my self-respect several years ago, "Mother, why would you put any substance in the opinions of people with whom you profoundly disagree?"

I know. But no one, no one, should be called ugly. No one should be judged as if a human slave at auction or cattle to be sold. All those industries to the contrary—fashion, diet, exercise, cosmetics, surgery, jewelry, medical, advertising, job market and insurance—I must not believe their falsehoods. Their bottom line would destroy me and countless others, most especially women.

Chapter 14

Screaming in the Face of the World, or What Does Acceptance Look Like?

"I'm sorry for you. I wish you could get to the place where you just say 'This is who I am' and let it go at that."

This was my therapist and friend speaking, saying almost *THE EXACT SAME WORDS TO ME* as she had said a year ago. Obviously, I am stuck.

Where I am stuck is in seeing myself as old, fat, and terribly unattractive. Looking in the mirror, I see myself with the same eyes with which I saw my sister Jane, eyes that tell me the reflection in the mirror is old, heavy, belligerent, white-haired, out of fashion, brittle so as to deflect any pity or criticism and to deny my own feelings and thoughts.

Going through one more bunch of photographs my husband brings home from a recent whatever, I race through them, only glancing at myself, old, heavy, unfashionable, looking angry, always talking or gesturing, as if to convince others I am unaware of any unattractiveness about myself.

Later, I go through the photographs once more, usually when my mood has shifted and I am feeling more secure and grounded. Then my appearance changes a little and I can look at myself with a bit more compassion, but I don't test that by going through the pictures a third time!

Last Saturday at the Women's AA meeting, a beautiful black woman who is on work release and cooking at the Governor's Mansion, told me about seeing a picture there of me in my lovely green inaugural dress. She said over and over again "You were so beautiful; you were so beautiful!" It was clear she meant no harm and her words did not cause that inner pain I am familiar with. Yet I wondered if she knew what her words meant: You were so beautiful *THEN*, certainly not now.

As I wrote in previous chapters, I feel buffeted, barraged, constantly hit with the culture's disgust of and criticism of fat women. Even one of my favorite meditation books, in a page about denial, says among other things, "Overeating causes obesity."

Several years ago I became uneasy with my friends and brilliant workshop leaders, Sidney and Suzanne Simon, for encouraging those women in workshops who vow to go home and join some weight loss program, and for joining in the group cheerleading for such promises. I wrote them a long, serious letter, after which we never discussed the issue.

I have to bite my tongue not to tell women in my Self-Esteem or Women and Aging workshops that on lists of risks to take or things "not to regret not having done before I die" *THEY MAY NOT PUT "LOSE 10 POUNDS."* Sometimes I just tell them that anyway, even though it's their list, not mine.

A friend sent me a *Washington Post* Style section article, July 10, 1995, by Iris Krasnow, headlined "Women at 50: Fit, Fulfilled & Blazing." I felt left-out and not-so-"blazing", at 65, gray-haired, heavy, even with my enormously fulfilling life.

Krasnow, herself 42, felt she was offering *Post* readers examples of becoming 50 that is something besides the beginning of a dowdy old age.

She reports on several women who maintain their beauty, youthful appearance, slim, shapely, and healthy bodies, and find new lovers and success in business. The article is illustrated with photographs of Katharine Hepburn at 88, the "ever pert" Sally Field at 48, Sophia Loren at 60, and Tina Turner at 56. Is it, I wonder, as difficult for other women as it feels to me, this barrage of famous, gorgeous women used as examples of what old age, or arriving at 50, looks like?

Clarissa Pinkola Estes, herself a large woman, and author of the vital and profound *Women Who Run with the Wolves*, Ballantine Books, 1993, is quoted in the Krasnow article about a woman not being able to command the culture we live in to change, but to "change her own attitude toward herself." Estes recommends, among her writings full of wisdom and courage, that we not accept the narrow cultural definition of happiness as coming from being a certain size or age or appearance.

In Chapter 6 of her runaway bestseller, *Finding One's Pack: Belonging as Blessing*, p. 185, Estes writes: "When culture narrowly defines what constitutes success or desirable perfection in anything—looks, height, strength, form, acquisitive power, economics, manliness, womanliness, good children, good behavior, religious belief—then corresponding mandates to measure oneself against these criteria are introjected into the psyches of all the members of that culture."

Estes uses the words "full-bore" and "all stops out" in advising women not to wait or hold "back to do anything . . . taking back her real life." Exhortations of old people to be full of pep, "up" about life, active, and god forbid, never without confidence, are mostly directed at old women, of whom there are more than old men. Being old for men has different, less harsh, restrictions. Such admonitions assume that we know, as we enter old age, what our "real life" is and have figured out how to live it.

Sometimes I feel sad, aware in old age of my own arrogance in even beginning to suggest to another how to live her life, in my writing and workshops. I imagine a buzzing, unthinking cloud of gnats flying about above the United States descending to pep-talk women from auditorium stages to "do it like me," life life "full bore," and "all stops out." Even as I need to attend to these words that describe life lived in all its suffering and glory by Estes, I must remember that they may sound hollow and pretentious to the woman mired in poverty, ill health, depression, besides in the invisibility of old age and shame of being fat.

Thousands of women, including me and several friends, find Estes' work enormously liberating—one can hardly open her book to a page that does not address eloquently the essential issue of women socialized not to be their true selves; my re-read of her splendid Chapter 7, "Joyous Body: The Wild Flesh" in *Women Who Run with the Wolves*, (Ballantine, 1992, 1995) filled me with exactly that—joy!

In a fine interview with Estes, by Isabella Wylde in the Winter 1994 *Radiance*, pp. 25, 30-31, 39, Estes equates maintaining "a weight that's less than her body would like to be" to "robbing women's creative life from them—to set them after a foolish task . . . It shows the separation of the person from their own soul life. I can't even imagine," Estes continues, "that we were put on the face of this Earth in order to be thin. I think most of us are here on a mission . . . to do helping and healing and discovery and creation. I think the idea of body size is a diversion and a distraction from the real work. The process of being here is the most important, and we must honor that with respect and love."

Krasnow leads off the concluding paragraph with a quote from journalist Elizabeth Kaye's new book *Mid-Life: Notes from the Halfway Mark* (Addison-Wesley), which speaks of "real loss that has taken place, a loss of youth poignantly mourned."

Kaye writes: ". . . agonizing over age is seen as a weakness that goes against popular feel-good culture." She maintains that without experiencing pain over lost youth, real growth cannot occur.

In my own *Women and Aging, Celebrating Ourselves,* and in speeches I am asked to give to women's groups, I quote the late Caroline Preston, first president of the Older Women's League in Seattle, who wrote as she was dying of cancer, that the "dark side" of growing old needed to be expressed, contradicting the "empowerment" theme.

"[Such] optimistic views of aging are as hard on us as our previous invisibility. We find ourselves yearning to be like people in these pictures and belabor ourselves for failing these role models. As I age, I marvel that we do as well as we do. The erosion of autonomy in aging is incessant . . . Often friends may comment on our apparent good mood . . . This can become a mandate to be cheerful at all costs lest we disappoint our well-meaning friends."

Often people in my classes and audiences do not wish to confront any of the losses or regrets of aging, finding me morose for suggesting such.

Two recent experiences left me gasping at what women contend with as they age, and in what our society expects us to look like.

One: After being extremely ill for three months with bacterial infections in my intestines, I hardly knew how to respond when two people commented that at least it was good I was losing weight. I felt lame to tell each that losing weight was not on my agenda, sick or well. They were silent at such heresy.

The other: Scheduled to speak at a woman's club, during the prebridge lunch of the club's oldest members, I quickly realized how untenable a situation it was. They did not want me there, many did not listen, several were rude; only later did I recognize that my error was as great as theirs: how dare I, and the committee, interrupt their visiting time, AND with someone 20 years younger who deigned to speak to them about growing old.

Betty Friedan counseled at her keynote address to an "Enduring Spirit, Women as We Age" conference sponsored by the University of Nebraska at Omaha College of Continuing Studies April 11, 1996, "If you don't cling desperately to the fountain of youth, you move into a new dimension of your being. You can be liberated from having to prove yourself in the sex and power games. You become more authentically yourself, wholly yourself, and you are free to risk new adventures, and not just rappeling down a cliff or river rafting, although that is a good metaphor."

She offered this wisdom to the standing-room-only audience: "It is not true that you love the way you did at 30 or you don't love at all. It's not true that you work the way you did at 30 or you don't work at all. It's not true that you need the power you had at 30 or 40 or you will be utterly powerless. We have to break through that either/or thinking. The third of life after 50 has to be seen as a new period of life on its own terms."

I applaud Betty Friedan's work and her courage in moving into a new place in her old age. I don't think we "become" anything, other than clones of our culture, the TV, the reigning sentiment, without an enormous amount of work, of risk. That requires turning away from what once gave us satisfaction and pride, giving up our hard-won place in the establishment, or recognizing that our goals have changed or can be affirmed by the growing size- and age-acceptance movements.

An old age spent competing, spent working on being "fit and fabulous and fifty," is staying addicted to the male gaze, to the patriarchal system we live in that values women for their appearance, that defines women in relation to men. To keep women's noses to that grindstone is basically one of keeping and getting them to be constant consumers of the products of the hundreds of billions of dollars of the appearance industries.

I am somewhat bothered by the "success and fame and power" issue illustrated by Krasnow's article. Would that we all were Katharine Hepburn, born rich, courageous liver of an independent life, great actress! Betty Friedan demonstrates enormous courage and intelligence in her life, and has faced and experienced her share of life's pain and loss. Maybe she is right, that we do *become* more authentically ourselves as we become less young, less sexually attractive, less addicted to what others think and say. We work to liberate ourselves from "the fountain of youth" or become sad at who we become, or we boast of our still-young bodies, still trying to please the male gaze.

How do I liberate myself from seeing myself with disgust, with this obsession with what I look like, with this seeming inability to see myself with love and affection?

My friend Linda, a large woman who dresses with extraordinary flair and style, whose jet black hair and beautiful coloring combine to make her striking and indeed beautiful, tells me about how she practices saying affirmations to herself every day. Even *I* lead self-esteem classes in which one session concentrates entirely on the things we tell ourselves that criticize, how we must fight back against this "self-hater," as Starhawk calls these voices.

That remedy seems too simple, too New Age, too shallow. But have I tried it? Do I look in the mirror and express appreciation for this self, for the life I experience in this marvelously functioning body? Do I take time to be naked in front of a mirror, getting to know this old fat body rather than just bemoaning it? Do I take risks in how I dress, sometimes appearing as the flamboyant self I long for? How often do I give myself time in a hot tub, swirling and playing in the restoring waters? Do I let this body dance, move, express itself? Have I bestirred myself to join the Friday night folk dancers in my town?

I find taped to a counter in my kitchen this obviously theologic but nevertheless powerful idea: Paul Tillich's definition of "the courage to be" is "the courage to accept oneself as accepted in spite of being unacceptable." Unacceptable to one's self, not to a dubious deity, I say.

Another of my favorite meditation books, *The Color of Light, Meditations for All of Us Living with AIDS* by Perry Tilleraas

(Hazelden Foundation, 1988), gives an unusual take on "Acceptance" on its July 3 page.

> Acceptance does not mean suffering. Suffering puts walls around pain, closes in on it, and tries to change it. Acceptance allows pain to move. Suffering, like self-pity, holds on to disturbing thoughts and keeps them hostage. Acceptance lets them pass. . . Acceptance stands at the top of the hill, faces the wind, throws back [its] shoulders and screams. Acceptance allows energy to move . . . doesn't mean we have to like [that person, place, or thing]. . . It's okay to make a fuss, even a big fuss. Acceptance means letting energy move. It means we're alive. . . Energy moves around me, past me, though me. I am changing.

That feels good. I don't have to pretend a thing. I can scream and yell and laugh and cry. I can move to get out of this stuck place. I do not want to spend whatever years I have left endlessly whining about what I look like. I truly want to find myself beautiful, without resorting to those tricks offered by the culture I live in that continue the myth that youth is possible for the old, that looking young *AND* thin is the most important issue for women.

I constantly and everywhere see beauty and grace in old women, in large women, in fat women, in women of all sizes and shapes and colors and ages and physical conditions. Now, how about in me too!

Chapter 15

Help!
The Avalanche Roars Down on Us!

Painfully obvious to me is that it is high time to batten down the hatches for the duration; it'll do no good to rail at the gods of our thin-obsessed culture, to demand acceptance of anyone but ourselves.

The media storm, the avalanche of stories about fat-reducing drugs, about thin being healthier for women, is going to drown us all. Tiny redemptions appear in the press, such as a fat-reducing drug having a down side; will thin still be in when it comes in a pill? They are only a barely audible signal bleating to those of us hunkered down, which send the valiant message that the rear-guard troops are still alive and resisting this takeover.

I've even lost track of which new breakthrough came first; sequence doesn't matter, only that the relentless pounding away continues against large and fat women. A September story from the *Seattle Post-Intelligencer* (reprinted in the September 21, 1995, *Omaha World-Herald*) reports a flutter against the tide: an article titled "Group Seeks to Boost Fat Peoples' Self-Esteem" reports from NAAFA's annual convention. They expected 350 to 400 members in Bellevue, Washington, a David against Goliath.

I do not suspect a conspiracy; one is not needed. That women are to be thin, that fat is not only ugly but morally bad, is as deeply imbedded in our culture as the notion that our country can do no wrong in its so-called benevolent domination of the rest of the world.

Ann Landers reported in September to a correspondent complaining about nine-year-olds talking about fat and skinny, discussing diets and addressing criticism to girls with "weight problems": "I see no realistic solution to this problem since the obsession to be pencil-thin is inherent in our culture. How unfortunate."

Ann Lander's words were strong and excellent, except "inherent." Does that mean it just came out of the ether and planted itself into our natures, and we are powerless over it? I wonder if she meant by "inherent" that such is inherent in a capitalist society organized for profit. Inherent suggests the passive voice to my ears, coming right out and not placing responsibility on the purveyors of "pencil-thin," such as the patriarchy, the media, all hierarchical institutions, gigantic industries such as fashion, cosmetics, surgery, insurance, medicine, dieting, exercise, and others that are less overt. My day of September 10, 1996, was immensely cheered to read powerful, in-your-face letters from fat women, from women furious at Ann Landers' advice to an "overweight" woman to get counseling. A woman in Milan, Minnesota, wrote, "Get a clue, Ann! There are fat people all over the world who are healthy and happy. They fight a constant battle to maintain their self-esteem against a barrage of misinformation promoted by people like you who keep saying we are unhealthy, unhappy, and emotionally distraught. There's nothing wrong with me, so what's YOUR problem?" I hope she was deluged with letters; such response indicates to me there is hope for different-sized people.

One should add to that enormously powerful list of institutions that profit from pencil-thin as a standard for women, the scientific community that announces to us the newly discovered hormone that regulates body fat so dramatically that obese laboratory mice given injections of it shed a third of their weight in two weeks. The obese mice—three times their norm, comparable to a 500-pound man, the *Los Angeles Times* (reprinted in the August 14, 1995, *Lincoln Journal-Star*) tells us—had a genetic defect that kept them from producing leptin, after which injections they started eating less, moving around more, generating more heat, and otherwise adjusting their thermostats to burning fat.

Los Angeles Times writer Terence Monmaney, writing of the fat-grabbing metabolism of human beings when famine was a constant threat, quotes as a caveat to this thin-hormone, Barbara J. Moore, a nutritionist and executive director of Shape Up America (I kid you not), a public-health education campaign. Moore said that most people are "*overweight* [emphasis mine] for simple, non-genetic reasons"—they eat too much and move around too little. She fears leptin-like drug users would lose out on the benefits of physical activity. I thought the mice ate less and moved around more. Never a chance too insignificant or convoluted to rant against the overeaters and couch potatoes. Cotton Mather had nothing on these modern-day moralists.

People are lining up to be volunteers for human testing with Amgen, Inc. a California-based pharmaceutical firm that bought rights to the protein. Phones rang off the hook, too, at Rockefeller University where researcher Jeffrey M. Friedman first cloned the OB gene, which makes leptin, and then isolated the protein itself. Amgen has yet to prove the safety of the protein or put a price on this drug with astronomical potential. Some overdosed mice have starved to death on leptin. Since leptin is digested in the stomach, it will have to be injected like insulin.

All the new writers use the word "obese" without any definition of it. Fat clinics, as we label thousands of such places, probably have lots of size 14 and 16 candidates, considered at least "overweight" if not "obese," desperate not to be dumped by their husband for a younger, thinner woman.

I talked to a vivacious, smart, radical woman this week; she and I agreed on so much of our similar work about aging women and appearances issues for women. Then she referred to her most successful sister, a woman sought after in her profession for teaching and advice, as "overweight." Large, confident, and successful in both her vocational and personal life, this woman is considered "overweight" by her family, who feel bad for her, which her sister described to me with regret. Although updated in the 1980s, height and weight tables on which many still base their diagnoses of "overweight," besides what we think someone looks like, are still calculated by an insurance company, Metropolitan Life of Indiana, without considering the range of size and weight that might be as healthy.

This conversation about the large, successful woman reminded me of the painful conversation I had with a friend who has a PhD, is a celebrated teacher, regular jogger, kayaker, canoer, and who lives in a supportive and loving partnership. Before making a recent visit to her large Italian family, her mother asked her by telephone if she would do her a favor. My friend asked "What?" with baited breath, knowing all the issues of conflict between herself and her Old World parents. "Could you lose ten pounds?" After all the years of her daughter's extraordinary achievements, I thought bitterly, and registered amazement and dismay at the depth and tenacity of the roots of how we fit into society, this antiwoman bias and hatred in our culture.

A Food and Drug Administration panel split just this week over whether or not to approve marketing dexfenfluramine, an obesity drug manufactured by Interneuron Pharmaceuticals. "A theoretical risk of brain damage made it too dangerous to use," reported the Associated Press from Rockville, Maryland (in *The Arizona Republic*, September 29, 1995). It has been shown to cause brain damage at very high doses in animals, prompting concern about how it would affect the thousands of Americans who might use it, even selling at 10 to 20 times lower doses than the animal tests.

One of the panel members on the losing side of the 5 to 3 vote, Dr. Nemat Borhani, told the panel, "We are dealing with a very severe epidemic of obesity" with no medical treatment. He persuaded the panel to vote on allowing the FDA to approve the drug with the "strict condition that Interneuron do massive studies of the first Americans to use it." Lack of a full panel put off this vote until the next day.

Brain damage? A drug untested on humans? One suspects a rush to make millions on the part of Interneuron, a company that is not alone in the drug manufacturing world anxious to produce chemicals to solve all living problems. Many of these anxieties are artificially produced by other industries wanting to get rich off our fears and phobias.

A new research study from the Harvard Medical School, reported in an Associated Press story in the September 14, 1995 *Lincoln Journal Star*, suggests, "Even mild to moderate overweight [for women] is associated with a substantial risk of premature death," says study director Dr. JoAnn E. Manson. That's a perfect example, if we need one, that such researchers are not talking about 500-pound men. Do they think we are getting out of hand, we who can cite equally solid studies that show that fat does not necessarily mean unhealthy, nor lead to an early death?

The researchers estimate, Associated Press writer Daniel Haney reports, that "weight is to blame for one-quarter of all deaths among middle-aged women . . . weight kills largely by increasing the risk of heart attacks and cancer, especially cancer of the colon, uterus, and breast."

I assume that this is an extensive, clinical study, yet flawed in some deeply troubling way, its information yet another vehicle with which to flog American women into concentrating almost entirely on their weight. A national disease exacerbated, women already obsessed told they may get fatal diseases if they do not become more obsessed.

My god, what is enough?

The news story concludes, "Just how fat is too fat is controversial. The government issued weight guidelines in 1990 that were up to 20 pounds higher than those listed in the Metropolitan Life tables, standard since 1959. Federal guidelines are being revised, and the recommended weights are likely to fall." Federal weight guidelines say women over age 35 and 5'5" can safely weight between 126 and 162 pounds, but the new research suggests anything over 119 is too much.

The doctor-reported caveats to the study, and the study's thin parts themselves, are buried in the final paragraphs of a long front-page story and carried on an inside page.

All of this information was followed by a Scripps Howard News Service report carried in the September 26, 1995, Scottsbluff, Nebraska, *Star-Herald*, of the latest study at Cornell University that concludes, according to Dr. David Levitsky, "the health risks of being moderately underweight are comparable to that of being quite overweight and look more serious than most people realize." The Cornell researchers found standard ideal weight tables too low by 15 pounds, because most have been developed by insurance companies from data collected on policy holders who don't represent the entire population.

Is Bosnia too painful and too complicated to contemplate, thus we are encouraged to navel-gaze and live in the illusion that we at least have control over something?

Weight Watchers wants me to "come back for only $9" and for-gives me for dropping out, even for gaining weight. "With every pound I lost, the better my life became. Soon I found a great new job and the love of my life, Jimmy. Even though I was 60 pounds from my goal, it didn't matter to him and he fell in love with *me*, and we married," reports Marianne. Did Marianne sign a prenuptial agree-ment to lose that final 60 pounds, so Jimmy could still be "in love with" her? Susan says, "I wanted to die with shame. I wasn't preg-nant . . . I was overweight . . . I've learned that it's not a shame to be overweight. It's only a shame to do nothing about it. . . I learned how to be in control . . . ."

My favorite entertainment on Tuesday nights is the extremely conservative *National Enquirer*, which used its normal flamboyant style to herald "Mom Loses 30 Years After Plastic Surgery Miracle," in an issue last spring. Before-and-after pictures with a "You Won't Believe Her Age!" sticker atop the after photograph show 70-year-old "English divorcee" and actress Catherine de Woolf, who "knocked decades off her age when she invested $11,000 on a 'plastic surgery vacation' to a clinic in Spain. . . . Catherine went under the scalpel at the famous Medici Clinic in Marbella, Spain. . . . 'I couldn't bear the way I looked and it was affecting my self-esteem . . . Now look at me. I can't stop looking in the mirror.'" That $11,000 vacation consisted of "a long incision across her forehead inside the hairline to lift facial skin and smooth out frown lines and other wrinkles . . . fat removed from bags under eyes and eyelids tightened, crow's feet disappeared after incisions were made in hairline to lift the skin . . . neck and jawline tightened by having loose skin cut away . . . silicone implants inserted in cheeks to fill out her gaunt look."

We have such trouble in this country being human and imperfect. We make Icarus fastening wings on his body and trying to fly to the sun look like a piker. Our attempts to soar above being human are vastly more subtle, ludicrous, and ultimately self-defeating, if not deadly.

Chapter 16

The Birds

The little birds came flocking across the country club driveway, flocking in their tiny glittery cocktail suits, their white stockings, their little low-heeled shoes, accompanied by their suited partners.

I felt like a butterfly pinned to the wall, caught by this flock of perfectly, properly dressed women flooding from cars driven by their husbands to the private club for the wedding reception of the daughter of an equally fashionable couple.

They fluttered, they smiled their charming smiles, they walked erect, sure of their plumage, proper little birds always. My husband and I and another couple were leaving the club after an early supper, unaware that we would cross the path of this social migration.

Lots of old college friends and acquaintances, who now live out of town, were back for this wedding reunion, and my lawyer/politician husband, whose establishment credentials are untarnished, greeted many of them with ease, fraternity brothers among them. The four of us were an island, an eddy in the river, the birds and their partners swirling around us.

A powerful searchlight of shame remembers for me only that I visited with a tall, handsome couple, she rail thin like all the other women, he as sturdy and wryly quiet as he was 40 years ago. They'd been ranchers since they left the university, successful ones from the looks of them. I kept wondering if she wore that large diamond on a necklace chain when she went into town for groceries, dressed in jeans, boots, and a shirt. Probably so.

He stood there silently, looking at me the entire time. Was he trying to remember who this was standing beside the man he remembered? Was he thinking, "My god, she's gotten fat!" Or was he just biding his time until the conversation stopped and he and his wife could move on to the reception? Not a word came from him, only the long looks I interpreted as puzzled.

I can't remember but I suspect the little birds talked in chirpy tones, as women do in public, maybe especially in the presence of men, maybe under the stress of having to be charming. Who knows? It is a kind of a "Hi there" chirp—cheery, smiley, pleasant, certifiable good-girl behavior.

A perfect portrait of the little bird, watching the men talk, smiling, listening, making unobtrusive appreciative comments, moving her head from one to the other, was captured for me at a meeting of law firms my husband belongs to. From across the room, I watched a woman I had loved talking to earlier that day, stand at tiny attention, feet properly together, between her husband and another man, being a perfect auxiliary, supportive, pleasant, attentive, to the men. At that biennial conference, it was easy to tell wives from women attorneys. Wives were heavier; less fashionably dressed, except for the occasional bird; older; and tended to listen, rather than talk, around the men.

In that flood of the wedding reception/college reunion birds and their mates, I never felt fatter, worse dressed or more socially out of place. Earlier, I'd put on some dress I consider nice for the occasion of an informal dinner at that upper-class, dress-up place, although the summery material billowed and I suspected my husband thought it made me look fatter than I am. Since I only wear Birkenstock shoes—flat, wide, sensible and comfortable—I didn't even have on little heels to give me a slightly fashionable look below my nearly ankle-length dress.

All my dresses are slightly billowy and long. I do not fit into nor qualify for the birds, who wear cocktail suits that end above the knee, little suits that are cut straight for the birdlike figures. De-rigueur white stockings make their bird-like legs look like a flock stepping along quickly, together.

Here I am, attacking my sisters, out of my ridiculous insecurities that, old and fat, I no longer belong to their club. When I did belong, I didn't think of it, the insouciance of the insider.

I know that I am making a scapegoat of being old and heavy to avoid insecurities that I have carried for a lifetime. That is one of the truths that can make me free, once I emotionally get hold of it, face the insecurities, not rail about our appearance-obsessed culture, and quit judging on appearance, too.

Still I cringe at the sight of the little birds, these flocks of women who exemplify the sarcastic words that Annie Lennox sings, "Keep young and beautiful so you'll be loved" (words by Al Dubin, music by Harry Warren, 1933). They are thin, fashionably dressed, adorned with "good" jewelry, their gray hair dyed or brushed with blond streaks or coifed into fashionable styles, socially adept, more often than not extroverted, married to a man successful in his profession. They can still maintain establishment credentials as camouflage.

Last fall, the *Omaha World-Herald* published two full newspaper pages of people attending the annual social ritual of the Ak-Sar-Ben Ball. Naturally, all the people pictured were prominent socially— which means money, then power, then old family. The makers of the women's gowns were mentioned, since this affair requires the women to purchase the most fashionable evening dress they can find—afford is probably not an issue.

What I noticed is that all the women were rail thin, all looking chic in what I'd guess were size 4 or 6, possibly size 8 or 10, gowns. Did no large women attend, out of more than 500 ballgoers? Did any heavy women refuse to be photographed or did the *Omaha World-Herald* photographers not select anyone who didn't look especially good, that is, certainly not fat?

Photographers may be a specially prejudiced lot. I remember, still with some pain, the man photographing our family of five at the Reflecting Pool on the Mall in Washington, DC, for our biannual portrait to send to my husband's constituents. That year I was fat and confused about my life, acting out in awkward, strange ways. Yet I knew no other way to behave than to keep up the front, do what I'd always done, in this case have our picture taken to be reproduced on thousands of postcards. As the photographer arranged us, he suggested one of the girls sit in front of me "to hide her fat," meaning me. I winced, not realizing until then that my size needed to be disguised, not realizing he had been trying to make me look better, and deeply embarrassed to have been singled out to be partially hidden.

Size is a class issue. Lower-class women don't have the time or money to spend on diets, exercise, new clothes, fancy hair-dos or makeup to make one look young and slim. Ak-Sar-Ben and the wedding reception at the country club are made up of upper class, and upper middle-class, almost entirely, white people. Occasionally, a black businessperson and/or an East Indian doctor may apply.

When we were in France at my husband's Rotary convention this summer, I longed for a glimpse of my stereotype of a European peasant woman, large, hard-working, earthy, real. I bet they don't greet the flu with happy thoughts of losing a few pounds for the suffering. I used to, until one of the counselors at Weight Watchers told me that flu-lost pounds come back on quickly. Possibly she didn't know that Weight Watchers pounds lost return in full and more, too. But not if one keeps coming and paying to Weight Watchers.

Thirty-three billion dollars a year is the latest estimate of what people spend in the weight-loss industry in the United States. As Jean Kilbourne says in her latest hard-hitting video, *Slim Hopes: Advertising and the Obsession with Thinness*, there's big profit to be made from making women feel bad about themselves.

I am no longer a consumer of the diet and weight-loss industry. Somedays I spend not one minute lamenting my lost size 10. I am beginning to thank my heavy body for its health and strength, its holding of me through life.

Yet caught in the flock of birds, the women who know how to be loved and admired, although willing captives in the women's prison of who you are is what you look like, your value determined by someone else, I felt bad about myself in comparison.

Who am I, in my heavy body, my long skirts, my unfashionable clothing, hair, and makeup, my unfashionable political work, my unfashionable everything self? Who am I outside the bounds set for me by the patriarchy, by all of our culture? Someone who has to criticize other women in order to exist and feel alright about myself? I hope not, yet I still do. Part of who I am is my appearance—old, heavy, white-haired, and worthy—even surrounded by flocks of the fashionable birds.

I love hearing the crows from up high in the trees, cawing, restless, flying high, said in an ancient legend to carry the souls of old women. I didn't grow up in the country where crows are considered pests. Hearing them settles me, calls me to some flock beyond the little birds, to both flocks of and solitary crows, who live on the margins of birds we favor, loud and outside our rules for nice pretty song birds.

Chapter 17

Why Do I Feel Like a Bull's Eye?

"Oh, you hear that all the time," my husband responded to my careless reporting to him of what has become, to me, the ultimate horror story of men's hatred of fat women.

The story came from my first class: a young woman told us her parents were divorcing, and when the mother asked the father why he was divorcing her, he took her hand, led her to a full-length mirror, and said: "Just *look* at yourself."

So is that common currency among the establishment my husband lives in? I suppose they even think they are justified, maybe even saying to one another, "If she really cared about herself or me and the kids, she wouldn't let herself go."

My recent journey through my middle-class American life includes horror stories ranging from the banal to the obscene.

A large woman and I sat together at a birthday tea. She told me she wanted to take my evening class, on "Women, Weight, and Appearances," but decided not to drive to the community college on the edge of town from her downtown apartment. She lives there alone, her husband of 27 years coming out as a gay man and choosing that life free of her.

Although she is struggling with bitterness and anger, she described to me how she stands up for herself, citing a recent incident in a doctor's office where she refused to be weighed, a routine of office procedures, when she was there for an examination for a specific disease, unrelated to her weight.

Yet she said to me, "I am going to take that pill." What pill? Isn't it dangerous? Why, I wondered, after she'd just told me how she doesn't let anyone criticize or demean her for her weight? Does she harbor the suspicions that if she had not gained weight, her ex-husband would not have been gay? Is she finding ways to hate herself under the barrage to her self-esteem of losing the partner with whom she had planned her old age? Of course, her behavior is deeply controlled by the myth fed to women, that she will feel better about herself, about her life, about everything, if she loses weight. Skeletal anorexic and bulimic women think so, too.

Getting dressed after a swim, I overheard women in the locker room having the usual conversation about their weight, size, appearance. A large, outgoing woman wanted us to know she had gained 100 pounds after "the brain tumor." She went on at some length about how nice she used to look, never once, even at my insistence, mentioning the good trade of life with extra pounds over death from a brain tumor, if those two circumstances of her life are indeed related.

As I checked into a local hospital for a minor procedure one morning, the admitting woman insisted we use the word "mature" to describe me, not old, even when I use old to describe myself. The week before I had led a three-hour workshop on women and aging at this same hospital, not that information from there would filter from the top floor auditorium down to the first floor. Even women in aging groups, and one or two women attending that hospital's aging program, brightly chirp to me after the workshop, "I am not going to get old."

Again in the same two-week period, I called long distance the brother of my old college roommate. I heard of her death, months after that fact, and wanted to talk to him about my old friend. A well-known Episcopal priest and author of several books, I pictured him sitting in his study as we talked.

My friend died in her sleep, having had a mastectomy the year before and a diagnosis of throat cancer early that summer. She was also a heavy smoker. Innocently, I questioned her brother, "So her heart just gave out in her sleep?"—from her various illnesses and her smoking, I meant.

"Oh, my god, she was obese, so obese," was his response. There was no autopsy so we both were guessing. His guess was that she died from weighing too much. I did not remember her as "obese" at a class reunion more than a year ago. I checked with another friend who attended that same reunion; she laughed at his description of his sister as "obese." "Heavens, no," she replied.

How sad, I thought. Even in death, we criticize large women. How sad that her brother is angry at her, undoubtedly considers her smoking, her alcoholism (from which she was in recovery), her messy housekeeping, and her weight to be moral failings for which she must be judged.

An old friend and I met for lunch the next week. She used the same word, over and over again, to describe both her close friend and business associate and that person's daughter. "Obese" she kept calling them, as if she had some pass from a doctor's office to decide who is just fat, who weighs more than average, and who is "obese." As if doctors have any precise definition, which they do not.

She brought me a birthday card with a photograph of four old women, holding hands, walking into the ocean. Three were rail thin and the fourth maybe—just maybe—a size 12. My friend pointed out the evidence of cellulite on their thighs, which she found a realistic portrayal of old women. Yup, I guess we all have it, or have surgeons perform indecent operations on our bodies to reduce its appearance. "Cellulite" is a word made up to shame women for aging skin and fat, to sell creams and potions to "get rid" of it, and to encourage surgery to remove such unattractive lumps on one's thighs.

There is a woman I see at my pool occasionally, severely disabled from a stroke that occurred on the operating table during liposuction surgery. Anecdotal evidence, I know.

A few years ago, in our state, a political maneuver found the woman lieutenant governor resigning to become head of economic development, and the governor appointing one of his cabinet heads to the Lieutenant Governor spot. The first Lieutenant Governor is older, slightly stout, and the new appointee young, rail thin, and fashionably beautiful. Both women are educated, professional, and thoroughly able to do many jobs.

I am still angry at this male ploy for political capital. I am convinced that the governor's political advisors picked a designer candidate to replace the older, less fashionable woman; and, for what might be an equally strong reason, hid in a department a woman whose strong dedication to feminist action might have interfered with the conservative male governor's political future. As a matter of fact, the head of economic development is a more powerful position; except any Lieutenant Governor is positioned to become governor.

It comes in waves, waves that assault any thoughtful person's desire to be all of herself, not just what she looks like. The assault comes from people whose values are fixated on the narrow, random, ever-changing, culturally approved, and based-on-male-gaze appearance of women and girls.

As I look back on the last ten days, I am not able to remember any such cluster of insults, of attacks on large and old women. Some days I am wildly sensitive and some days less so. We become especially vulnerable around our natal birthdays, a wise old friend used to caution, and that may certainly be true in the case of this fall's plethora of slings and arrows.

I have ads clipped from the Sunday papers two weeks in a row. One, from a board-certified dermatologist, shows a charming eight-year-old girl and says, "Remember when you were the picture of health and beauty? No matter what your age, you can have healthier, lovelier-looking skin." It suggests eliminating lines and wrinkles, surgery for other conditions, and concludes that the doctor "can help you and your family." Does that suggest that other members of your family need surgery, too, or that they will benefit if you have "healthier, lovelier-looking skin" and eliminate lines and wrinkles? I am sure the dermatologists are not suggesting that men and children have surgery on their faces in order to appear more appealing to women, and to help their families!

The next Sunday, an ad caught my eye with sketches of trim versus bulging thighs. "After the holidays, give yourself a gift," said the headline, recommending "healthy diet, regular exercise, and *in office liposuction (for the resistant areas)*." This information seminar is presented by two dermatologist doctors.

More recently, a larger ad jumped out of the newspaper at me. It was an illustration of a birthday cake and contained this headline: "I may be 'middle-aged' but I'm not going down without a fight!" For "baby boomers [who] have reached (gasp!) MIDDLE AGE," these same dermatologists offer "Silktouch™" laser for erasing wrinkles, creases and acne scars, and in-office liposuction for removing unsightly areas of fat." "Free seminars"—another marketing tool—are offered at the bottom of the ad. Harumph, I say. Come in and let us describe in glowing terms how we can cut up your body and make you look younger longer.

Marilyn Gardner wrote in *The Christian Science Monitor* (November 16, 1995) about the latest offering from Neiman Marcus. "For $3,000, social planners . . . will arrange an 'unbelievably awesome' event for 10 little girls—a 'supermodel slumber party.'" A glossy catalog explains that young guests "will don matching gowns and slippers and snack on Neiman Marcus party treats as Chanel makeup artists provide 'makeovers.'"

Gardner concludes, "these pint-sized beauties will be getting an early lesson in the high cost of looking great. For adults who believe you can never be too rich or too thin, the new corollary seems to be: You can never be too young to be preoccupied with your looks."

One woman who missed some class sessions of the six-week "Women, Weight, and Appearance" wrote me this week:

> I still have mixed feelings on how to accept myself *as is*. I feel I still should change myself—this could come from a friendship I had with a girl when I was very young. Her mother was bound that this friend would be a model (clothes.) She was very much 'overweight' (I know I shouldn't use that word), and after having her tonsils out at the age of around 12, she (on purpose) lost a lot of weight and became very obsessive about 'thinness.' Since we were friends, I too thought I was overweight, which has been with me most of my life. I struggle each day with the thought of being thin like I was prior to my marriage. It's something I will probably live with for the rest of my life.

What a prophecy for American women! We blame ourselves for our addiction to thinness, in addition to criticizing ourselves for not being thin.

Surely we can laugh over this ad in this morning's Sunday paper, asking "Are you tired of being Fat?" I say how about, "Are you tired of this culture being obsessed with fat?" This "secret" solution, discovered by millions of women in Asia, [eating rice? laboring long and hard hours? genetically programmed for less body fat?] is

"SOFT SEAWEED SLIMMING SOAP. Just lather up and watch the fat go down the drain. Only $10.50 per bar. Results may vary depending upon individual."

We'll buy anything to stop the suffering caused by the constant judgment about our, about all women's size, shape, weight, and appearance.

How can an ordinary person change—and maintain a strong sense of one's worth—amid the daily, hourly assault on ourselves carried on by demands internalized, and what spews into our universe from friends, greeting cards, television, newspapers, magazines, store windows, stores, doctors, insurance companies, surgeons, clothing manufacturers, and men, just to name a few?

We can honor and like ourselves, reclaim our real selves, and free up energy for the real issues of our lives only with daily, hourly affirmative action in solidarity with other women, and by exploring and exploding the mythology and misogyny underneath this cultural deprivation. We can fight back in productive ways against the society that bombards us from every direction with insistence that we be thin and obsessed with our looks, and tells us we are not okay if we resist that imprisonment.

Chapter 18

Weight Watchers:
How They Want Us Back!

In the past year, I received in the mail a Weight Watchers pamphlet, exhorting me to "Come Back." (It reminds me of the Catholic Church's commercial about "coming home to the Church," triggering and distributing guilt as usual.) I had been a dutiful attender of Weight Watcher meetings for several months a few years back, winning a weight-loss award, and still not liking my size at 131 pounds. After that came the final weight gain.

Weight Watchers is still after the backsliders—that is, people who no longer show up on their membership rolls—with the zeal of the missionary.

Their advertising come-ons, however, are more overtly sexual than those of people selling religious salvation. Weight Watchers is selling salvation by looks, not by good deeds, except as we in this country consider losing weight an especially good deed and by faith in its promises.

The woman model on the back cover of this latest brochure is tan, thin, young, stretched out on top of a white stucco structure, head to the sky, one hand to the throat, the other concealed in her lap by her flouncy white dress, her right nipple showing through the thin summery material, her back arched.

The woman is having an orgasm and wouldn't you if you'd just lost weight? Losing weight means you can *have* multiple frequent orgasms because you will attract the man of your dreams. You can also be tan because you'll be living in some glamorous vacation place, and will wear a little white dress that shows off your tan, your thick brunette hair, and your breasts.

Leading up to this orgasm of appearance-making-everything-better is an early strategy in the Weight Watchers solicitation: "So when's your baby due? an innocent stranger asked me as I was watering my garden. I thought I would die . . . I wasn't pregnant—I was overweight." Tell me.

There is no consideration of the rudeness of strangers, only the unstated cultural rule that comments on people's fat are considered appropriate, even to our face or certainly within our hearing. Nor is any attack considered too mean to turn into, inside ourselves, that great old line of devastation: "What did I do to deserve this? What did I do wrong? How can I be different so they'll not attack me?" I remember the shame of that same experience—of people thinking I was pregnant. I guess I've always had a stomach waiting to pop out. In those days before menopause, I *knew* I had done something wrong, actually was committing a sin by becoming so heavy that I embarrassed my friends when they beamed to me, "Oh, you're pregnant!"

I know about that. As I described in the first chapter, when I was obviously an old woman, a male acquaintance patted my stomach and asked derisively, "On the nest, are we?" So such comments are not restricted to women able to bear children.

The second "come-on" by Weight Watchers says, "Make the decision that can change you life forever, Ruth!" Losing weight is to offer everything in our culture. "With Weight Watchers on your side, Ruth, anything is possible." Technology allows them to design a booklet with my name conveniently and frequently inserted, making me understand that the issue is me.

On a further page of this slick-paper, several colors of ink, oversize brochure is a photograph of a darling young woman in a little black dress, holding a bouquet of roses, arm around her loving hunk's white-coated, open-shirted body, her head coyly on his shoulder, both grinning to beat the band. Weight Watchers tells me,

> There's Big News in Lincoln, NE! Now Weight Watchers has even more of what you need to succeed! More personal attention. More care. More flexible choices . . . so Weight Watchers suits your lifestyle even more, Ruth! You really owe it to yourself to come back . . . today!

The facing page shows a woman playing football with two young boys shouting "This time, I'll have the energy to keep up with my kids."

It is as if fat women do not play with their kids, have no energy, do not attract men, look like they are pregnant, have low self-esteem, have let themselves go, and cannot wear attractive clothes.

Going on, Weight Watchers quotes a tiny woman cavorting in the tide on a beach: "This time, I'm going to feel good in my own skin." Yes, by having less for my skin to cover, by reducing the space I take up in this world. God forbid that we should consider feeling good in our skin because we are healthy, active, sane, productive, creative, loving, thoughtful women.

Before-and-after photographs and incredibly shiny, colorful, mouth-watering pictures of food are leading illustrations in this sales pitch. You can buy the Weight Watchers food plan, video, guidebook, magazine, body tube exerciser, walking belt and squeeze bottle, complete exercise book, food companion, fast food companion, family dining companion, fat and fiber selection trackers—whatever those are—activity plan, and special savings coupons, all for just three payments of $36.65, plus $8.95 shipping and handling.

This Weight Watchers "at home" package is pitched to women who are "actually too embarrassed to attend a meeting. . . . Her self-esteem had ebbed to the point where she actually convinced herself she couldn't return to the meeting room." Self-shunning, indeed. After losing 52 pounds, Patty "came back" and became a "meeting leader so she could share her phenomenal experience with others."

This $109.95 plus shipping and handling does not include buying the Weight Watchers food so artfully shown in the pages, the description of which includes such evocative words as "international selections," "form a healthy relationship with pleasure," "luscious," "exotic world flavors," and "something you can really get passionate about."

We're working up to those orgasms—sex through food.

The next to last page is the killer pitch for Weight Watchers frozen desserts: "Deny yourself nothing. Life is short . . . it should be sweet . . . How can you resist? Enjoy, guilt-free, with gusto!" So if you think losing weight and being wonderful is about denial or limits or boredom, or even, the goddesses forbid, starvation, think again. You can have it all!

The final before-and-after photographs on the inside back cover show a fat woman with pale skin sitting on the grass, her legs apart, a loose T-shirt on top, smiling, and that same woman after losing 105 pounds, standing, fashionably posed, wearing a sharp red blouse, tan trousers, and black pumps, *beaming.*

"I went all the way with Weight Watchers . . . this time, you can too!"

"All the way" is an old sexual phrase meaning going beyond petting or making out to having sexual intercourse. Weight Watchers is not kidding. Every word is carefully chosen . . . to lead you to the ultimate orgasm provided for only $9 per session "plus Weight Watchers Guarantee" of new sessions, new food plan, more personal service" *AND* what? Weight loss? Men? Unbridled happiness? A wonderful life? Great sex? A good job? Adoring and constant attention? A nice home? Deep sleep? Adoration of your children? Vacations of your dreams? Fame and fortune?

Weight loss for women is offered as the road to all of the above, even in the "gathering dark," (Tony Kushner's epilogue to *Angels in America* [Theatre Communications Group, 1993, p. 158]), in this world of greed, war, environmental destruction, and the growing chasm between the rich and the poor.

Kushner writes, "Together we organize the world for ourselves, or at least we organize our understanding of it; we reflect it, refract it, criticize it, grieve over its savagery; and we help each other to discern, amidst the gathering dark, paths of resistance, pockets of peace, and places from whence hope may be plausibly expected."

From Kushner's words at the end of two awesome evenings of theater, "a gay fantasia on national themes," AIDS in America, and the lives of gay men, I take hope. As we live "amidst the gathering dark," I reject the seductions of a Weight Watchers brochure that begs me to "come back" to being an object of approval from people whose values I decry. I need all my strength and spirit to find those "paths of resistance, pockets of peace, and places from whence hope may be plausibly expected."

Chapter 19

Don't Raise Your Head—
They're Still Shooting!

It doesn't stop; the barrage keeps coming.

At least *Cathy*, comic strip character who obsesses about men, eating, and shopping, is making slight fun of artificial fat and mice that lose weight. And I can laugh at the advertisement for "silktouch laser technology" that shows a big, homely dog and says, "Some think highly of their wrinkles."

However, even famous, wise health guru Deepak Chopra has weighed in to the battle against upsetting someone by what you look like. His latest brochure in the mail offers to "help you achieve your ideal weight," with the old 30-day trial "complete mind/body approach to weight loss," complete with a two-week supply of OptiMetabolize herbal tablets. Eight lessons are available on audio-cassettes, with an accompanying Workbook and a Satisfaction Meter.

I can just see the Chopra promotion team, sifting through what attracts America's attention these days and, not needing to be brain surgeons, figuring out that losing weight is the prime national obsession/goal.

Of course, this thoughtful Indian medical doctor, renowned in mind/body medicine, would be advertised as offering "lose weight *naturally*." A headline on a four-color, oversized, slick-paper pamphlet illustrated with a human silhouette emerging behind an open zipper, boasts, "You can literally change your body as effortlessly as you change your clothes."

I like Chopra's work a great deal, once paying $36 and driving 60 miles to hear him lecture on the secrets of not aging. There my friend and I learned no secrets of not aging but heard Dr. Chopra's familiar and wise discussion of meditation and other facets of healthy living.

The "free body-type quiz" enclosed lets you figure out if you show characteristics of Vasa dosha, Pitta dosha, or Kapha dosha, under what I assume are Ayurvedic medicine systems, and that the 30-day trial weight loss plan will fully explore these body types. This plays on that old fascination to take one more "who am I?" test.

"Look forward to a future filled with perfect health and bliss . . . say goodbye to weight problems forever . . . simply by listening . . . harness your own inner intelligence to bring your mind and body into perfect balance . . . teach your body to convert food into positive energy instead of fat" are some of the hyperbolic promises made in the promotion literature.

Chopra does not emphasize set-point or healthy eating and exercise, but blatantly offers "the natural weight *loss* technique that releases the *slender*, energetic, *confident* you hidden inside!"

In concert with the national war on fat, the myth that thin means confident, that thin is preferred, and that bliss comes through weight loss are all maintained, even by this degreed, distinguished man surrounded with the aura of mystery suggested by his Indian heritage and Ayurvedic medicine background, his stunning public presence, and his charismatic personality.

A stack of current advertisements, all culled from ordinary midwest newspapers and not from slick national magazines, herald a "new liposuction technique" that "removes more fat and speeds recovery." Accompanied by line drawings of "target areas," such as "outer thighs (saddlebags), inner thighs, hips, abdomen, flanks (lovehandles), upper arms, back, neck/chin, knees, ankles, male breasts, waist, buttocks [did they miss any body parts?]," this surgeon's ad labels his office the "tumescent liposuction centre."

"Centre" seems more cosmopolitan than "center," I suppose. This "revolutionary" procedure "involves the installation of a dilute anesthetic solution into the areas to be sculpted (tumescence) eliminating the need for a general anesthetic . . . [and] uses smaller instruments to minimize bruising, bleeding, scarring and soreness."

For "areas resistant to exercise and diet," this cutting of the body is hailed as "the solution to your problem areas." I would have thought problem areas to be places in the world where wars are waged, famine rages, people are hungry and tortured, where the rich get richer and the poor get poorer, rather than any "imperfections" of my body.

An ad that caught my eye, a modest offering in the slick magazine *Washington*, suggests that "When your faces ages faster than you do," the Austin-Weston Center for cosmetic surgery in McLean, Virginia, is the place to go.

In that same venue of power, where appearance carries heftier clout than elsewhere, *The Washington Post National Weekly Edition* (January 3-9, 1994) reports that the "90s promise to be boom years for tucks, weaves, and bobs" [aren't those cute words!] in the Washington, DC area, which "now supports the highest per-capita ratio of board-certified plastic surgeons in the country—higher even than New York and California." Is appearance more important to the business of U.S. government than ideas and energy, compassion and commitment?

The Post article authored by Jonathan Mahler reports from the American Academy of Cosmetic Surgery, "1.5 million cosmetic procedures were done in 1992; the Academy estimates procedures will be up at least 10 percent" in 1994. In 1994, according to the Academy, 2,084,317 women had cosmetic surgery. The most popular operations were vein, eyelid, and nose surgery; chemical peels; and liposuction. When "health reform will make other medical specialties less profitable . . . [for] young doctors looking to cash in . . . plastic surgery is one of the few paths still paved with gold. Because the strictly cosmetic [unnecessary] procedures aren't reimbursable, there is no need for messy paperwork . . . . Many offices even take credit cards."

"A study in November by economists at the University of Texas and Michigan State University . . . . documents a correlation between perceived physical attractiveness and financial success," this essential guide to our nation's power structures reports.

This is just the tip of the iceberg long researched and written about by Esther Rothblum, PhD, chair of women's studies and assistant professor of psychology at the University of Vermont. Dr. Rothblum has led several rigorous studies demonstrating prejudice against large and fat women in employment and other areas. With Laura S. Brown, PhD, clinical psychologist and associate professor of psychology at the University of Washington at Seattle, she edited *Overcoming Fear of Fat*, a series of professional articles that challenge cultural stereotypes of attractiveness for women, especially among feminist therapists.

Introducing *Fear of Fat*, the editors write:

> Fat oppression is hatred and discrimination against fat people, primarily fat women, solely because of their body size. It is the stigmatization of being fat, the terror of fat, the rationale for a thousand diets and an equal number of compulsive exercise programs. It is the equation of fat with being out-of-control, with laziness, with deeply-rooted pathology, with ugliness. It is . . . sexism in action . . . a catalyst for energy-draining self-hatred.

Wisely, the articles "challenge the notion that fat equals pathology." The researchers' aim is "to disconnect the issues of food intake and eating disorders from those of weight." Their perspective is "that being fat is simply one variant of human size, not an indication of disordered eating." It is amazing how people automatically think the issue is food and eating when I mention my work with weight and appearance issues for women.

Fear of Fat is one of the few books on women and fat that does not approach size as the problem; rather it approaches prejudice against fat as the problem. Hurrah!

Had I read all of Rothblum's work before writing these chapters, I could not even have started, since her work is so comprehensive, highly researched, and informed, and covers the territory of women and fat in all its personal and political manifestations.

Her in-depth study and surveys of the field include "Women and Weight: Fad and Fiction"; "Lesbians and Physical Appearance: Which Model Applies?"; "The Stigma of Women's Weight: Social and Economic Realities"; "Women and Weight: An International Perspective"; "Social Interactions of Obese and Nonobese Women"; "Effects of Clients' Obesity and Gender on the Therapy Judgments of Psychologists"; and "I'll Die for the Revolution But Don't Ask Me Not to Diet: Feminism and the Continuing Stigmatization of Obesity." This last is an extraordinarily comprehensive study and brilliant analysis, written in plain language, that plumbs the breadth and depths of this issue.

In *Confronting the Failure of Behavioral and Dietary Treatments for Obesity*, David Garner of Michigan State University and now eating disorder psychologist at Central Behavioral Health Care, Toledo, Ohio, and Susan Wooley of University of Cincinnati, remark of results of their studies in *Clinical Psychology Review Vol. II* (p. 991):

> . . . to remain cognizant of the social context within which obese people have lived, receiving weight loss advice from the health care establishment and encouragement to diet from family, friends, and media, and the weight loss industry. They have long believed that in order to feel good about themselves, they must lose weight. Giving up weight loss as a goal may be viewed as a surrender to self-loathing and relinquishment of hope for a degree of self-acceptance that most thin people take for granted. Thus, a *non-weight loss alternative* would need to be explored in a gradual and sensitive manner *without the expectation that it will be readily accepted"* (emphasis mine). (pp. 727-780)

No wonder that first "Women, Weight, and Appearance" class series in the fall of 1995 was so hard!

These researchers accept as obesity a scheme of definition relative to norms, as mild (20 to 40 percent overweight), moderate (41 to 100 percent overweight), or severe (more than 100 percent overweight). They note "these definitions are all arbitrary in the sense that they define the condition using cutoff points along a normal distribution of body weight or fat, without reference to etiology or disease." Those standards we all know for overweight and underweight, even the revised Metropolitan Life tables we see in doctors and insurance offices and libraries, were originally based on white, upper-class males living in the eastern United States. Today's adjusted charts are still flawed.

My own local paper, the *Lincoln Journal Star*, began the new year (1996) with a huge page feature on "Liposuction: new technique makes it easier and less painful." Nowhere in reporter David Swartzlander's story was there mention, or even a hint, that one need not nor should not have such painful surgeries done on one's body and face. It was entirely an advertisement for the "dermatologic" surgeon partners quoted, the reporter writing such lines as, "Don't sweat it . . . lose the fat without pumping the iron. Don't suck it in, suck it out. Stick a skinny, sticky-like wand *[wand!]* inside your-self, turn on the Hoover and vacuum up a tub of lard. It can be done in less than four hours in a doctor's office and by June, you'll get admiring stares from the opposite sex . . . ."

Such pie-in-the-sky offers horrify and deeply disturb me; equally do promotions for "olestra," the Procter & Gamble latest miracle that lets an artificial fat molecule pass right through the body. Having barely endured gall bladder surgery two years ago, I would not eat something that takes vitamins and nutrients out of my body, along with the artificial fat, and that also causes diarrhea, to which I am occasionally subject, more so now than before the surgery. Imagine doing that to one's body—knowingly eating food laced with olestra (is it supposed to sound like a Greek goddess?)—and enduring loss of health?

What caused the Food and Drug Administration to approve this billion dollar cash cow for P&G? It was approved in the face of advice of experts such as Michael Jacobson of the Center for Science in the Public Interest, who said, "It will cause everything from diarrhea to cancer, heart disease and blindness" (January 1, 1996, *Omaha World-Herald).*

"Americans will serve as guinea pigs, without their consent, in a massive uncontrolled experiment," wrote Meir Stampfer, epidemiology and nutrition professor at the Harvard School of Public Health, in a guest column in the *Boston Globe*, January 21, 1996, "This 'dieter's dream' may become a true nightmare" (p. 65).

"Long-term use of the recently-approved diet drug Redux substantially raises the risk of developing a rare, life-threatening lung condition," *The Washington Post* news service reported on Aug. 29, 1996, according to a report by an international team of scientists. The Food and Drug Administration has asked the drug's American marketer, Wyeth-Ayerst Laboratories, to make labeling changes to better inform patients and doctors about the increased risk of using Redux. The article continued, "The FDA underscored that the drug should not be used for 'cosmetic' weight loss. 'The take-home message is that only people with serious obesity should get a prescription for Redux or any other anorectic (diet) drug,' said George Blackburn, co-director for the National Institutes of Health's Obesity Nutrition Research Center in Boston."

Some good news *does* surface in this most recent batch of clippings, articles, and books that have shaped my journey this year, and
to which I cling as a life raft in this sea of hatred and control of
women and their bodies.

After the Olympic display of teensy female athletes, the Men-
ninger Eating Disorders Program in Topeka, Kansas reported,

> At least 10 per cent of female athletes suffer from eating disor-
> ders and 50 per cent more are at high risk for developing a
> problem. The rate of eating disorders among female athletes is
> nearly twice that of other young women. . . for several reasons,
> including striving to be perfect, high self-expectations, persis-
> tence and being goal oriented. Those with eating disorders that
> begin in childhood can face problems as adults, such as growth
> retardation, a deficit in bone density, delayed or interrupted
> puberty and structural abnormalities of the brain.

Such a price to pay for money and fame!

The Scripps Howard News Service reported late in 1995, from a
study conducted by David Levitsky, Cornell nutritional sciences and
psychology professor, that "the health risks of being 20 to 30
pounds overweight are exaggerated . . . being moderately underweight may be a greater health risk than most people suspect."
Levitsky said, "We found that people who were 20 to 30 pounds
overweight were not more likely to die over a 30-year period than
average-weight persons." His findings were based on an analysis of
19 large studies that involved 357,000 men and 249,000 women.

Ellen Goodman's February 18, 1994 column in *The Lincoln Star*
uses the case of TV anchor Kathleen Sullivan who "had gotten fat"
and now pitches for Weight Watchers, telling us "she only wanted to
lose the last 12 pounds for my health." Goodman retorts, "Show me
a woman who only wants to be thin for her health and I'll show you
a man who buys *Playboy* just to read the interview."

Goodman writes of the appalling statistics of women and young
girls on diets, how women would rather be dead than fat, no more
indisputable than the evidence of women starting to smoke and
refusing to quit, based on gaining weight, and how "we've become
much more conscious of what it costs women emotionally to play"
in the losing sport of dieting. She cites "a poll in last month's

Esquire that half of the 18- to 25-year-old women proclaimed that they would rather be dead than fat;" and from *Failing at Fairness*, a recent education book, "girls and women discuss losing weight the same way boys and men talk about sports. I suppose it's true."

"The shame of being fat is now accompanied by a shame of being ashamed," Goodman observes.

I understand well, and with chagrin, this polarization our objectification produces. Tipper Gore, wife of Vice President Al Gore, appeared on Jay Leno's *Tonight Show* one night in August of this summer (1996) to promote her new book of photographs. As she came on camera, I *immediately* said to myself, "Oh, she's gained weight. And is wearing black (always black!) slacks and a full tailored jacket to minimize that." I was appalled at my still current and functioning membership in the Criticize-Women-for-Their-Appearance Club. I thought I'd given it up, trying hard not to pay my dues anymore. As I continued to watch Tipper and Jay talk, I was soon struck with what a smart, thoughtful, perceptive, lovely woman she is.

An article by Daniel Goleman, a *New York Times* writer, in the April 3, 1995, *Lincoln Journal* looked like good news, headlined "Program helps people face the fat." But the first two sentences clear up that misperception by reporting a new treatment "to ease the psychological suffering associated with being overweight . . . not meant to discourage people from trying to lose weight, nor to deny the very real increased health risks that added pounds bring. Instead it seeks to ease emotional suffering." I suspect that's a realistic caveat, since researchers do not want to interfere with the weight problems or obsessions of, say, diabetics and people with heart disease.

In the new book *What Do You See When You Look in the Mirror? The New Body-Image Therapy for Women and Men* (Bantam, 1995)— what a heart-rending title—author Dr. Thomas Cash, psychologist at Old Dominion University in Richmond, Virginia, insists, "We say, do the healthy things—and one of those is to learn to accept your body in a world that does not." A study run by Dr. James C. Rosen, psychologist at the University of Vermont, "focused on freeing [51 women in the program] from self-reproach, endless rumination about appearance and their reluctance to appear in public." As if we made it all up all by ourselves.

Some of the "treatment" included "small group discussions of experiences where they were shamed and criticized for their weight; countering their own thoughts of self-deprecation and judgment; spending time alone studying their body in a mirror without bad-mouthing their body; and becoming more revealing of their bodies in public to get over their fears about being judged."

Those strategies, all productive of an increased sense of self, are part of the journey we took in that six-week class last fall, but without the clinical structure and with the important addition of long and fruitful discussions about the institutionalization of weight and fat oppression.

Always alert to this issue of women and weight, Ellen Goodman reports again in the June 11, 1996 *Lincoln Journal Star* about model Trish Goff appearing in the British edition of *Vogue*: "In the anatomical world of supermodels, Trish Goff has arrived to make Linda Evangelista look pudgy." Giving a brief history of the "skeletal look," Goodman writes of Twiggy, "Kate Moss waifed into the limelight at 100 pounds spread over her 5-foot-7-inch frame . . . Kristen McMenamy showed up in ads looking as if her only nutrition was the Diet Sprite she was promoting . . . last summer, vigilantes were scrawling graffiti over skinny billboard bodies: 'I'm so Hungry . . . Please Give Me A Cheeseburger.'"

Goodman writes, "For one sane moment, the Swiss watch company Omega pulled its ad from *Vogue* on the moral grounds that the incredible, shrinking models were encouraging eating disorders among young women readers." She decries that the Omega chair then recanted his stand, saying, "It is not in anybody's interest to influence the editorial position of any given media." Goodman wonders how this could be cast as a serious matter of free speech without serious tongue in cheek "First Amendment vs. Anorexia."

Goodman continues, "The parameters of weight gain are narrower and the price is higher. Annie Morton, co-star in *Vogue's* superslim issue, insists, 'I am not that thin.' . . . Is it any wonder that half the 9-year-old girls in this country diet?" She concludes, "The editorial position of the fashion world? You can read it in another generation of girls growing up in painfully hostile relationship to their bodies. Trish Goff is just another skeleton in the closet."

Keeping nine-year-olds on their diets is certainly encouraged by the news story that tells us the Miss Universe Pageant denies reports that the reigning beauty queen is eating her way out of the crown. (Associated Press, Caracas, Venezuela, published in the *Lincoln Journal Star*, August 21, 1996). U.S. and Venezuelan media recently reported that "Miss Universe Alicia Machado had been ordered to shed 20 pounds in two weeks or lose her title. At 5'7", Miss Machado weighed 113 pounds when she won the crown in May, 1996. She now weights 130 pounds because of her confessed weakness for chocolate, pasta, and corn pancakes, according to news reports." Marta Fajardo insisted her 19-year-old daughter had four wisdom teeth pulled, causing her face to swell. And of course pageant officials called the rumors "completely absurd. We don't put her on a scale and march her around. She's never had a weight problem. She's a beautiful girl."

Pauline Uchmanowicz, professor of rhetoric, composition and cultural studies at Wayne State University in Detroit, writes in the October 1995 *Z Magazine* about "Babes in Toyland: Disney culture and lifestyles of over consumption."

> The structural parallelism that links these dolls [Disney and Barbie dolls] should serve to remind us how the body has been technologized under media capitalism, made to appear as compatible with market forces as the components of interactive software," she warns, and points out that "Unlike feminist discourses that focus on the emancipation of the body, Barbie and Disney dolls symbolize disciplinary and regulatory controls exerted on the bodies of entire populations through what Michel Foucault calls big-power; for example, through institutional mechanisms related to health, pregnancy, life expectancy and psychological examinations.

Comedienne and TV talk-show host Rosie O'Donnell calls herself "fat, happy—and I don't want a man," having to explain to the world via a July 23, 1996, issue of the *National Enquirer* since she breaks the rules of the appearance police with her 5'7" body weighing 185 pounds. "I'm not going to diet again—ever! I'm tired of this ridiculous preoccupation American women have for their weight . . . . It's all for men. It's a male conspiracy."

Laurie Stone writes applause for O'Donnell's show in the July 9, 1996 *Village Voice,* comparing her to "large women of daytime— Oprah, Carnie Wilson, and ex-fatty Ricki Lake [who] are humiliated by their bodies. O'Donnell calls herself fat and neither weeps nor apologizes for liking food. She isn't about to trade her authority for a seat at a 12-step sisterhood. Internal voices don't censor her . . . . O'Donnell is Joan Rivers without the self-loathing. . . . Another day Donny Osmond calls her fat . . . she nails his boorishness . . . Rosie, clearly, has made friends in entertainment, and audiences are responding with similar affection for her big, smart, heartfelt, unembarrassed presence . . . independent, urban, unmarried, imposing."

A story reprinted from the zine *Fat!So?* tells of a fat woman searching for a compassionate doctor. She finds a doctor who concentrates almost entirely on the woman losing weight over and over again, forgetting the X rays and discussions of possible lung cancer. This "real-life tale from the weight wars" encourages me to order *Fat!So?* at $12/year (four issues) at Box 423464, San Francisco, CA 94142.

In the interstices between *Fat!So?* and Foucault, there are many antidotes for this disease if we search them out, not enough obviously to stop the onslaught, but perhaps enough to keep us from being devoured by this monster of perfectionism, of control, of denial, of greed, of abuse of who we truly are.

SECTION III:
TIME TO MOVE ON

Chapter 20

Love Letters

I keep my car radio tuned to stations that play jazz. That ordinary nurturing routine became a serendipitous correspondence, an opening into another world one spring (an incident I alluded to in Chapter 7) in which I heard old jazz musician and orchestra leader Preston Love criticize Della Reese for being "obese" on KIOS-FM, Omaha.

Outraged that singer Della Reese was not honored by fellow jazz musician Preston Love for her talent and success, I continued to hear him define her as "letting herself go" and "just eating too much." Love explained that he had just started his ten-week diet and the only reason for weighing "too much" was overeating.

My fury increased as I wrote to KIOS-FM: "The male gaze is vicious and perpetuates a demeaning and cruel falsehood—that we are what we look like to them—onto the lives of women. I would hope KIOS-FM's artists would not participate in such calumny."

Not surprisingly, Preston Love, an African-American man long renowned in musical circles and especially in Nebraska for "being from here," wrote back to advise me to listen to his response the next week, and said further,

> *No*, Della Reese is NOT attractive as she is now and this is said unanimously by all those who know her, including her colleagues. Of course they say it privately, but why not publicly. This certainly does not imply any "attack" upon her. Yet all who read your letter regard yours [as] an attack upon me. I regard yours as the "calumny" in this situation.
>
> And, please, for God's sake, don't try to inject the *male-female* or gender thing into this. It has no application here. I would say the same thing about her overeating and her physi-

cal appearance if I was a female or, conversely, if she were a male. There is nothing wrong with keeping one's self reasonably attractive and in good physical condition or at least reasonably so.

I met Della Reese in San Antonio, Texas in 1957 . . . She was then a fine physical specimen, and she is a "travesty" of that as she appears today. Of course, I had not the slightest interest in her as the male chauvinist you imply all men are, but I do have good VISION. I expressed an opinion on "Love Notes" [his radio show] that I will continue to have without the slightest intent to demean nor ridicule her.

He concluded with "regards [to your husband] whom I have always been a big 'fan' and supporter of." I got the message—there is one person in your family I like!

Recognizing that raising consciousness will not happen while I am making someone mad and grateful that he cared enough to answer my letter, I wrote back to Preston Love.

The trouble with keeping "one's self reasonably attractive and in good physical condition" is that who gets to define those terms? Our culture has an ever-changing, very narrow window of what is 'attractive' for women; there were times when voluptuous women were considered the most "attractive." And "in good physical condition" is terribly subjective. Charley [my husband] minds his own diabetes, and I mind my own high cholesterol, and we try not to judge each other's efforts to maintain our health as best we can.

I suspect that lots of people don't consider people with physical disabilities attractive, which is pretty hard on and unfair to such people. The whole point of the powerful story *Elephant Man* is that a deformed body housed a beautiful person, but only a very few could see that.

However, how can you say what you do about Della Reese, and at the same time say you have no intent to demean nor ridicule her? If calling her "not attractive" does "not imply any attack upon her" what do you call it? She might feel differently about that if you were to say such things directly to her. And do you think that speaking "publicly" about your idea of Della

Reese as "travesty" is any better than colleagues speaking thus privately? What justifies our criticism of one another?

Thanks for writing back. Maybe we can learn from each other.

PS: I think of Mahalia Jackson, Ella Fitzgerald, and Rosemary Clooney, great singers all, and wonder if their weight enters into your opinion of the splendid women they are.

Preston Love and I wrote to each other one more time; he did not choose to continue this dialogue after my last letter. Perhaps having such a demanding pen pal was not possible for his life; perhaps he felt we had come to some understanding—or not—and could let it go at that. I am genuinely grateful for our dialogue by letter.

Preston's last letter offered this:

Apparently the somewhat difference of our philosophies is the cause for your misunderstanding of my motive in making the comments about a woman's physique. My statement was spontaneous and hardly malicious but mainly meant as a COMPARISON between the person I first saw in 1957 and the person whom I see on television and in magazines now.

The standards of beauty and "attractiveness" are pretty well defined which has nothing to do with their intrinsic qualities. . . even the definition of "beauty" can be very subjective and personal.

Naturally we can't hold a person responsible for physical deterioration or changes brought about by age, pathological illnesses or accidents, but neglect of one's anatomy such as overeating and failure to get proper exercise can be remedied easily enough . . . In Ella's case, her debilitating illness has nearly "destroyed" her once healthy physique . . . I don't think Rosemary Clooney's appearance was enhanced by her great weight gains and in the case of Mahalia, I never knew her to look any different from her last years.

. . . every person alive is going to have opinions and reflections about everything we observe in life and I won't promise that I will never make a casual or spontaneous remark about things or people . . .

. . . only yesterday, a racetrack "associate" said to me. "Well, Preston, I hear you will be 74 years old on April 26. You are no longer young and handsome." He went on to "kid" me about my advanced age and my increased weight, all of which I found very TRUE and humorous. I was not in the least offended, but should curb my enormous penchant for sweets and other "goodies."

As for Della, maybe her physical changes are a blessing in disguise or an asset, since her career really "took off" in recent years. Hollywood has long been known for seeing all black women as another Aunt Jemina or Hattie McDaniels. Maybe the Hollywood of that day would have found it impossible to cast McDaniels (*Gone with the Wind*) and Louise Beavers in any other roles except the stereotypes of the day . . . both were excellent actresses. This wasn't limited just to our female blacks. Look back to those movies of the time and how they portrayed the black MAN same as with the females—how demeaning.

I wrote back to Preston:

I would be offended if a friend said "Well, Ruth, you are no longer young and pretty." Frankly I cannot imagine being comfortable hearing someone "kid" me about my advanced age and my increased weight. That's a critical statement, whether meant for a man or a woman; maybe it was just teasing— obviously neither of us is young. But "handsome" is *so* subjective. And the struggles of age and a changing body shape are difficult enough without someone making fun of us. Does that mean they are perfect according to our culture's standards? How do we justify that someone's appearance is no longer pleasing to *ME*?

In the conclusion to her "Ageism and the Politics of Beauty," in the April 1990 *Broomstick* [no longer in publication, alas], Cynthia Rich writes: [after discussing photographs of Septima Clark and Georgia O'Keefe when they were old women], "Our task is to learn, not to look insultingly beyond these features to a soul we can celebrate, but instead of take in these bodies as part of these souls—exciting, individual, beautiful.

After quoting that passage to Preston Love, I wrote, "Weight gain and loss, and body shape and size, [are] determined by genes and metabolism; that dieting causes one to gain more weight; that chronic dieting causes more health problems than fat; that fat people and thin people eat pretty much the same; that fat is not necessarily unhealthy and that fat people can and do lead healthy and productive lives, even joyous lives except for the prejudice against their appearance by others."

I concluded, "Thank you for educating me about how perhaps Della Reese's career may have been elevated by her weight gain, since Hollywood and/or our culture may want black women to fit the Aunt Jemina stereotype. And also for your remarks about how demeaning is the portrayal of the black man in many aspects of our culture. You have experienced much of what I have yet to learn and understand and be aware of. Thanks for trusting that I am able to become more conscious."

I am glad for this encounter, glad for even the misunderstandings between Preston and myself, and especially grateful that we can communicate across our differences, more able thus to celebrate them and come to know each other.

Chapter 21

Raw Courage
in the Face of Horror Stories

Overwhelmed is how I felt that first night of class. Almost unable to focus on the evening's agenda, I struggled to stay upright against the tidal waves of horror sweeping over me.

Eight women and I gathered—two hours on six Tuesday nights—to examine Women, Weight and Appearance. I have led such groups before, not recently, however, and not since I've done so much more research on this subject of how women are treated in the United States, based on what they look like.

Almost accidentally, I interrupted the schedule I'd drawn up for that first evening and laughingly suggested we share "the worst thing anyone ever said to you." What I can remember from the deep sadness and anger that coursed over us all is:

A very large woman reported that 20 years ago she had intestinal bypass surgery, designed to make her lose weight, followed by a stomach stapling—I recoil in horror at the very thought—after which she lost *not a single pound*. One out of ten people die from such operations. What we allow to be done to ourselves, besides that of the damaging, painful, rude, thoughtless things people say.

Seated next to her, another large woman told of her high-school nickname: Fat, Ugly, Bitch, the acronym of which she was called and described by in her high-school yearbook.

A tiny young woman, who herself had struggled with anorexia, then told that she'd encouraged her "overweight" mother to come to class but "her self-esteem is too low," especially since her parents are divorcing. She bravely told us that when her mother asked her father why he was divorcing her, he led her to a full-length mirror and said, "*Just* look at yourself"—A cruel new twist on the old story of men telling their wives "I'll divorce you if you get fat." I felt as if that husband had driven a stake—a big, splintery stake—into his wife's heart.

My complaints pale into insignificance in the face of such mutilation of women, although I resist the comparative gratitude process. People often remark to anyone complaining about aging to consider the alternative. Indeed. But thinking about death and dying does not specifically minister to the things about aging we need to change, celebrate, and mourn.

Two older women (one of whom is in a second marriage) both reported stories of being the outsider in their families because they have gained weight and are no longer among the thin and physically and psychologically elite. We need not look too far from home to find evidence of both unconscious and intentional ranking of women—even within a family—according to their weight, size, and appearance.

How much can we learn, how many times can we share, how much community can we build, how many assertive actions can we take to overcome seeing ourselves as unattractive in this youth and thin-obsessed culture?

That night I felt like a person drowning under the tide of hatred and cruelty inflicted on women and which we as the oppressed have learned to inflict on ourselves, internalizing the oppressor.

Just a few weeks ago, as a friend and I left a restaurant after lunch, I was greeted by a male acquaintance, a well-known professor, who was waiting for a table with his date, a much younger woman, with this question, "Are you being a good girl?" he asked me.

Now I cannot even remember what I said to him as I stood there in shock at such idiocy. I certainly have had countless discussions in my head of what I should have or needed to or wished I'd said to him.

"I haven't been a girl since I was 16 and what do you mean by good?" I know what he meant—a sexually loaded term applied to women, à la the tacky saying "If you can't be good, be careful," which is a cultural warning not to have sex but if you do, don't get pregnant; that is, use birth control.

Was he so full of his adolescent pride at dating a younger woman, at being sexually active since his wife's death, without the guilt of her presence marring his good time, was he so stuck in his own stuff that upon seeing a grown woman, an old woman, a heavy woman, he thought it cute or appropriate or flattering to greet her with "Are you being a good girl?"

When I confessed my inability to think of something to say, my luncheon friend pointed out that the professor, too, was at a loss for words. That would be the kind interpretation, that he was simply nonplussed, saying a stupid thing since he couldn't think of how to say hello. As Sylvia says, it's so hard to teach them their lines!

My other recent encounter, nowhere near as painful as the terrible sadness reported by the women in class, yet also disturbing, came as I ate lunch with a group of women, prior to being the main speaker. Frequently I speak to women's groups on "Women and Aging," sponsored by the Nebraska Humanities Committee resource bureau.

In that talk, as in my book *Women and Aging: Celebrating Ourselves* (Haworth Press 1992), I tell women that we must take affirmative action in old age in order not to be victims of the cultural rule that tells us to be caretakers, sexually attractive, or a Mother Teresa, in order to be valued as old women. I give lots of examples of what our culture does to us unless we fight back, and despite my morose self, people find my talk entertaining and occasionally enlightening.

The woman seated to my right was extolling the virtues of Sun City West where she and her husband spend the winter. "We even have pom-pom girls," she thrilled, "and they go everywhere." She described two groups of still-thin old women, one that forms a performing dance troop, and the other group of old women who entertain with their pom-pom act.

I suspect part of the audience's fun is in seeing old women make fools of themselves, acting like high schoolers. Not only was I a cheerleader in high school, but have spent a lot of my life cheerleading at my politician-husband's side and being active in various auxiliaries to his organizations and his career. I have to resist being one today, desperately needing my energy for my own life, not to dress up another's, navigating that fine line between support and codependence.

I took a deep breath and replied to this bearer of pom-pom tales that "Being a pom-pom girl is not something I've ever wished for myself in old age." Miraculously, I left it at that. To each her own, I truly believe. My path is not necessarily right for another.

Across the table a woman smiled and said, "I was wondering how you were going to respond to that." I grinned back at her, savoring this moment of knowing together that no encounter on our aging journey is equally without its difficulty and/or growth possibilities.

Columnist Ellen Goodman writes one of her strongest columns in the August 1, 1995, *Lincoln Star*, about the pop psychology alliterations normative to Gail Sheehy, who chronicles our passages, often segueing from cute phrases into shallow suggestions and solutions. Goodman calls Sheehy a "Chirpy Cheerer-upper." Calling Sheehy's *New Passages* (Random House, 1995) "a stone soup of a book," she decries such pop psychology: "You're not getting older, you're getting happier!" or "Each moment is like a snowflake" and "sageing" instead of aging. Sheehy bases her book on life stories of aging people that Goodman calls "not shallow but plumbed at exactly the same lack of depth. . . . How much time can someone in their Sage Seventies spend with someone who believes that 'each new awakening can jump us ahead to a higher curve in the road up the mountain of self-transcendence'. . . I imagine that we find more wisdom in biography than in pep talk. The irony in this sequel is that the tone, the style, the level of insight is unchanged from the 19-year-old original *Passages*."

Goodman sarcastically makes up her own labels—Fabulous Fun, Galloping Giggles, and the bull's eye, Chirpy Cheerer-upper—and then writes wisely, "At some point in life, we want to go deep. . . . a real longing to hear from people ahead of us how they endure and thrive." Some women thrive by being pom-pom girls in a city built and maintained for old people. Thank god I am drawn to neither— being a pom-pom girl nor living in any such place.

My children used to call me Eeyore, the melancholy donkey in *Winnie-the-Pooh*. Yet part of the work I am called to write and teach is what I call the *Chop Wood, Carry Water* school, the realities of life, its exigencies and dailiness, and how we endure and thrive therein.

Later that first Tuesday night, when I was less overcome with horror and sorrow, I marveled at the kind of raw courage demanded of women who do not fit the random, ever-changing, irrational, insane, life-destroying image of attractive, at women who choose to free themselves from the iron-barred prison of what we look like to another is who we are.

Chapter 22

Breaking Free

For the first four weeks of the class "Women, Weight, and Appearance," we labored under an emotional smothering, of feeling there was no way out of this female prison. Toward the end, we felt lighter, seeing a ray of hope at the end of this tunnel in which we are trapped by our culture and to which we intentionally turned our attention to see if and how we could free ourselves.

It was an experiment for all nine of us, especially the six of us who showed up every week, read every handout, read books, watched videos, and did individual investigation and reflection.

I had hoped and planned that there would be a progression for us, from feeling bad about our size—whether anorexic, large, or fat—to feeling good, to accepting ourselves exactly as we are, with not a single hidden thought of someday losing weight again. It is unrealistic, I realized as the classes went along, that a cultural norm can be overcome in a matter of weeks. It is, indeed, a lifelong journey.

There was, in fact, a cumulative progression in our attitudes, which could be discerned by looking back. Yet after each class we were not exactly bursting with hope, either for ourselves or for the culture we live in.

My old teacher, Sidney B. Simon, used to tell us that our faces need to reflect the truth of our lives, and that a sad or questioning face was often that of a person on a brave journey of understanding themselves, of searching for his or her true path. The ever-smiling person, he felt, is either choosing to stay on life's surface or hiding a heart full of pain. For years I've showed my values-realization classes the full-face photographs of Jerry Rubin and Abbey Hoffman: both old war resisters now dead; Rubin appears insouciant, blatantly looking into the camera, well-dressed, living his former radical life as a networker of people; Hoffman looks scruffy, sad, searching, more cognizant of the reality he chose to work to change, those demons and his own finally taking his life.

At the first meeting, we talked about what brought us to this unusual class and what our expectations were. An unplanned riotous, painful time of sharing "horror stories" interrupted the planned agenda, that spontaneous occurrence obviously essential for our work. We needed to name our pain, tell each other over and over again, finding commonality, outrage, and humor in our stories. Elizabeth O'Connor, writer and therapist living in community with *The Church of the Savior* in Washington, DC, most of her adult life, reminds us that we tell our stories until we are healed.

I try to condense my own outrage, and rationale for these classes, into a few sentences:

Despite the gains of the women's movement, women are still judged by what they look like, men by what they do.

That standard of judgment forms a tiny window of acceptability, which is random, ever-changing, arbitrary, irrational, based on "the male gaze" (Heilbrun), tenets of patriarchy, and *sexual* attractiveness.

Women are disempowered by being coerced into spending their energies on dieting, obsessive exercise, makeup, hair style and hair color, clothing, and body size, shape, and weight.

We are taught to and *do* use our bodies as scapegoats for the real issues of our lives that need attention.

Surrounded as we are by TV, billboards, magazines, newspapers, store windows, store clerks, ubiquitous and constant advertising, doctors and insurance company advice, and our own internalized appearance police, those of us who care not to be robots must take strong, daily, affirmative action to value ourselves differently.

Without specific steps to reject a negating and negative picture of ourselves, and to build a healthy self, we are at the mercy of those voices that say we are fat, unattractive, lazy, sloppy, piggy, sexless, weak-willed, or obsessed with our bodies. Those same voices frequently blame us, its victims, for constantly changing ourselves in order to fit an external definition of what is okay.

In class, we each took about five minutes to give a brief biography—when we first started dieting, when we first realized we couldn't get thin enough, who influenced those decisions, what we did about them, when we first started taking diet pills, when our clothing sizes changed, and how we feel about all of that right now. Everyone felt some despair, some hopelessness, some dismay about their size, their efforts to change that, what their families say to them, and what they say to themselves.

These feelings and descriptions match closely how we describe thin and fat. As I've pointed out before, thin means all the good things, fat all the bad. Although they are more pervasive and vicious, our adjectives for thin and fat correspond closely with the words we use to describe young and old. Young gets all the "good" adjectives—active, resourceful, energetic, attractive, powerful—and old gets the "bad" words—tired, sexless, whiny, dumpy, strange. In polite company, we only call someone old or fat in their absence. A caveat to this manners rule is that we feel free to assume that all myths about all fat people are true, and that they need and want our advice about how and what not to eat and to lose weight. Any comments that insinuate or emphasize young and thin, even if our remarks are obvious falsehoods, are accepted as pleasure.

A quick brainstorming of adjectives to describe THIN produced these words: pretty, chic, good, athletic, healthy, disciplined, attractive, desirable, ideal, lithe. "Skinny" and "smoker" were the only negative words we thought of during those few minutes.

For FAT, we listed ugly, sloppy, slow, pretty face, out of control, poochy, dumpy, undisciplined, faceless, jolly, lazy, self-indulgent, funny, victim, and mound.

That first night we used large sheets of newsprint and magic markers to sketch our bodies, in silence. We showed our drawings to one another and described what we were thinking as we drew. To a psychologist, this would surely be self-revealing. To us, it was a gentle way of seeing how we see ourselves, and together finding something tender about what we think we look like.

Only one woman was brave or insouciant enough to post her drawing at home on the refrigerator for all in her family, especially her husband, to see.

Again in silence, we wrote our diet history; this charting exercise takes more than one attempt. The first go at it simply primes the pump of our memories. We remember more as the weeks go on of *years* of trying to change our bodies' sizes and weights.

This journal writing brings up lots of feelings, and although we did not review our entire list with one another, we talk about how these memories affect us. Revealing and purposeful, it is more poignant than we expected.

In the too-short time we took for writing this first diet history memory, I listed the following: dieting as a matter of course among my mother and two sisters and I; my size in junior high and high school and how important that was; always knowing about every new diet, and talking with friends about their experiences with each; losing ten pounds after Dad died, the better to "catch" my husband; three pregnancies; eating carrots and celery that last week before my first child was born when my weight reached its limit (for those times, 1958) and my blood pressure went up; vomiting to relieve my stomach of the nausea of alcohol abuse; in retrospect, consistently thin before bearing children; gaining the maximum weight for pregnancy when three months pregnant with my second child, those first two births 16 months apart; using diet pills as a young mother; priding myself on being as thin as my peer group in early married years, even after bearing three children; becoming fat at the end of my active alcoholism, ashamed more of my appearance than of my acting-out behavior; one fall, smartly, I thought then, existing on skim milk mixed with scotch whiskey, and gruyere cheese; being a 32-year heavy smoker, once quitting for two weeks when a doctor labeled my lungs pre-emphysemic, and starting again because I immediately began to gain weight; leaving alcohol treatment, feeling slim and attractive again; aware of beginning to gain weight after trips to Nicaragua and Peru in the mid 1980s, and my mother's death in 1991; those strange, lonely, prideful months in Weight Watchers; beginning not to deny myself any food or eating when I felt hungry; and finding stores that carry more sizes for large women.

Those memories do not each recall a specific diet, but each does refer to the constant obsession with our size, what we looked like according to the culture's standards, what we ate, and how best to continue to achieve that acceptable appearance. The "we" I use refers to family and peer groups. There was never, ever, a concern about health or what our obsessive behaviors were doing to our health. Yet I did indulge in considerable criticism of anyone heavier than size 10. Women's eyes are smartly trained to be able to tell you another women's dress size in seconds.

At the next class, we planned to discuss the main body messages we received growing up, and those we currently absorb from the media surrounding us, how large women are depicted therein, and what examples of sexism, ageism, looksism, and ableism we observed in the week ahead.

We were also to examine ourselves without clothing at least once in a full-length mirror, trying not to judge—hair, fat, body shape, facial features, skin spots, all those things we see first when we see ourselves.

A three-hour class, with time for a short break, would undoubtedly work better than a two-hour class, since all the subjects and all the strategies provoked more discussion than I imagined. Women desperately need to talk, to share with one another, their life-long struggle to match some externalized ideal, internalized for most of our lives by virtue of being born female in this culture.

Each session would benefit, I now realize, from a positive ending, that is, some short, verbal process that lets us laugh, lets off pressure, lets us know how brave we are to undertake this journey, and that sends us off into the night armed with the conviction that we are doing something good for ourselves, as we labor to hack our way through the bars of our prisons.

Each class's ending could be as simple as naming one body-positive thing and vowing to carry it out in the next week—for example, not to criticize one's reflection in a mirror; wear a comfortable, favorite garment to work or to a party; go out in public *not* trying to cover up one's size—wear a belt, a shirt tucked in, etc.; write in a journal one way you subvert yourself in conversation with others. The next week we could report back to the group about how our positive effort went, without judgment, simply observing what we did, what worked, what didn't, what we want to incorporate into our daily routines.

The head of the continuing education department at the community college that offered these classes questioned the number of handouts I asked his office to copy. The entire packet was thick as a manuscript; to treat it as a workbook students purchase for the class would solve this problem. The brave work toward a new definition of women represented in these handout essays and articles forms a parallel course by itself, reading such literature one of the vital and enduring acts of sustenance and liberation that I cherish on my own journey.

Chapter 23

Trudging Through

One of the most helpful things we did in class began our second week together: we wrote a body/appearance review of our last 24 hours.

That exercise seems small, simple, even unimportant, but it became enormously revealing and comforting. There is so much we try to deny, even though denial is, in fact, often a workable survival technique. But to look things right in the face, to go through as opposed to use energy to go the long way around, will ground us in our present reality, provide us with a powerful sense that we are not pretending.

My first 24-hour review, without my intentionally doing anything in order to include it on that list, recorded the following: preparing that night's class and dressing easily for that; little kids at the swimming pool staring at my naked body; the pain of a partially collapsed lung; not liking my hair, especially as I got ready to go to a twice-weekly poetry class at a university; a semi-conscious decision not to be naked in my office as I worked that morning—and that pull between wanting to and feeling foolish even to think about it; a conversation after poetry class with the instructor, which focused on our love of language in which I felt myself totally "enough"—no thoughts of my appearance during that radiant time; a mental image of my quite thin friend while we talked on the long distance telephone; being overwhelmed in class by women's stories; and the energy I felt taking my daily walk.

That's an amazing amount of information to recall, to list, to process, ripe for reflection. Surprisingly, writing a 24-hour body review became one of our favorite things to do. When I remembered, we spent ten minutes each class writing it in silence. If we had continued to meet, in the form of a support group, for instance, such an exercise would be an excellent, automatic way to move into the work of reclaiming ourselves and our bodies.

Each week we reviewed our homework; this second week and in the other sessions, too, we had show-and-tell time that included examples of how women's weight and size is treated in various media—advertising, TV shows, magazines, store windows, etc.

We briefly discussed the handouts we'd read between the last class and the current one. This learning would have been better served by discussing only one article per week, or leaving time at the end of the class for comments on which reading piece spoke most directly to each person.

Occasionally, we went around the room, each person saying, "My name is _____. I am a beautiful woman. I am here because _____." This was hard for everyone to say; try saying "I am a beautiful woman" and watch your own inner critic go to work.

That premise needed to be reinforced each week, as did the direction of our work, that we are exploring giving up diets, not holding in our stomachs; learning not to obsess in any way about our appearance, weight, shape, size, or food; and experimenting with not covering up or changing all those things we are told are wrong about our physical selves.

A discussion of the messages we received growing up; about old people; the differently abled; big, fat women; lesbian women; and women of color was surprisingly revealing, painful, and broad.

We didn't cast blame on whomever we learned such prejudices from. We just talked about them. We *all* remembered several examples of what prejudice was appropriate in our families and neighborhoods and how we participated in it, mostly without taking any responsibility that it was wrong or hurtful to others.

In my house, fat people were absolutely anathema and we spoke disparagingly about some of them, particularly if they were fat women. I suspect being fat was one of the major cardinal sins in my immediate family. There were few people of color in my small midwestern town: one African American in my high-school class, a few Native Americans, and lots of Mexicans who had come to the North Platte River valley in the early 1900s to work in the beet fields.

One of my most delightful *and* painful adult experiences came a few years ago as I flew across Nebraska to lead a workshop in that old hometown. The handsome Mexican man seated across the aisle was returning from a meeting of the Equal Employment Opportunity Commission in the state capital, Lincoln, to which he had been appointed by the governor. As we talked, Manuel Escamilla told me about a family reunion he would attend that summer—that of his third-generation Mexican family in the valley, still headed by that very old original patriarch. He guessed there were hundreds of such family reunions held in western Nebraska. Joyfully, I listened to his stories, and at the same time was torn up inside at my part in the prejudice against his people as I grew up alongside them in Scottsbluff. Funny, to have that inner track going on, while listening to his words. He might have had some inner thoughts of his own. Now I wish I'd simply told him what I was feeling so we could have discussed that old prejudice.

Our memories in class about lesbian women or homosexual men were almost nonexistent, except for remembering snide comments about the women high-school gym teachers who lived together. Men could be unmarried and considered just bachelor uncles. Unmarried women were more suspect since all women were supposed to be married at a certain age, or else there was something wrong with them, *unless* of course they were taking care of old parents. This is a reverse discrimination from the early 1900s when women who lived together were accepted, some such arrangements once called Boston marriages.

Differently abled people, how did we view them, we who then considered ourselves the standard from which to judge others? I am terribly aware that I am not using the words we used—Rooshians for the German-Russians, Negroes for Blacks, Indians for Native Americans. Did we say crippled? I do not know. I do remember using the word "gimp." Besides our pity, what name did we invent for people with what we called a "harelip"? That must have been the common word as opposed to the medical term, one in use back then, which I do not find in a dictionary.

There was a fat boy in my grade whose last name seated him directly behind me in our alphabetical grade school and junior-high years. We liked him and felt sorry for him. His intelligence and humor served him well and lessened our patronizing attitude toward him. Anyone with a physical disability we simply tried to ignore. It was not good taste to comment on or draw attention to the withered arm, the polio-weakened body, the birthmarked face, the harelip. Pretending such infirmities (wrong word!) were not there was like turning a great spotlight on them; of course we discussed such differences and disabilities in private, among our undeformed selves.

The women in class did focus on the *main body messages* we received growing up—including that one all girls learn early: to hold in your stomach. Stand up straight. Keep your legs together. Always wear a slip. Always wear a bra. Girdles and garter belts were de rigueur underwear in my growing up years. Today I cannot imagine sucking, squeezing, and pulling one's body into one of those terrible latex or rubber tubes we thought essential to our appearance.

I should not have been surprised or upset to read in the December 5, 1996 *Omaha World-Herald* newspaper about "New Undergarments Reshape Extra Weight." Around we go, back to "the fashion industry . . . hawking a few bits of Lycra, underwire, and lace to camouflage the damage done by gluttony." It is *your gluttony*, understand, that causes companies to produce new undergarments "that would allow a woman to eat to excess and then smooth out any resulting bumps and bulges by stuffing herself into a tight Lycra casing."

The company BodySlimmers by Nancy Ganz and Wonderbra market bodyshapers, foundation garments, and girdles, answering "feminists who fought the good fight against stays and corsets" by Ganz saying "Women are so liberated, so free, so empowered, that they can take back those constricting garments."

Writer Robin Givhan of *The Washington Post* makes fun of such undergarments and not at all subtly emphasizes women's "gluttony," eating "to excess," concluding that "a cookie-consuming body at rest gets fat . . . that sucking in a gut doesn't make it go away," attributing guilt and sloth to that woman who even needs such underclothing.

Marketing something new or refigured is the bottom line, as is that profound truth that you can make women buy something by making them feel bad about themselves. I suspect Givhan is promoting exercise programs like hers that have kept her above the fray and able to snicker at large women.

Lots of people grow up being told they are ugly, unattractive, will never get a man, are freckled-faced (as if it were a bad thing), and that their _____ (thighs, legs, bosoms, arms, stomach, bottom, etc.) are too fat or thin or incorrectly shaped. Faces come in for their share of criticism, from the occasional bucktoothed to noses labeled too big or too small or crooked. In the small, midwestern edge of western America, conventional and conservative farm and ranch community in which I grew up in the 1940s, there was only ever one word applied to Eleanor Roosevelt, the active, controversial, brave wife of President Franklin Delano Roosevelt: ugly. That's how we evidenced our disdain for her, diminished her accomplishments, pointing out she did not fit the first requirement of a wife, especially the wife of a public person.

Then we sing-song to one another that stupid, untrue saying: Sticks and stones can break my bones but words will never hurt me. Hah!

All those years that I reminded my children to "get your hair out of your eyes and clean up your room," I was sure that my job as a parent was to change those things about them that made me uncomfortable, never once examining if that was appropriate for them.

Comments on hip and waist size and bust measurements were common currency in my childhood and teenage years, as were the rules that a nice woman does not dye her hair or wear fingernail polish or much makeup, nor does she swing her hips. We were supposed to adhere to that fine, nearly invisible line between too much, not enough, and just right. Goldilocks and her porridge and beds! Women and girls were supposed to be sexually attractive, but not look as if they were trying to be—that intersection between virgin and whore, narrowing to invisibility whenever criticism and demonizing of women fits someone's agenda. It's the same as the Dallas Cowboys cheerleader mystique of today—look, be sexually aroused, but DO NOT TOUCH. I love Cornelia Otis Skinner's old words: "Women's virtue is man's greatest invention" which jumped out at me this morning from Anne Wilson Schaef's *Meditations for WOMEN Who Do Too Much* (Harper & Row, 1990, August 29).

Skinny as a broomstick, if you turn sidewise we couldn't see you, fat as a pig, big as a barn, wide as a house, twiggy, roly-poly—ordinary expressions we used with impunity.

We took time to review our diet histories, and discovered we'd thought of many more things to add to them. Every week, I brought in that week's current deluge of newspaper clippings, reports from the front in the war on fat. Each week's plenteous supply was certain evidence of the epidemic of the disease of judging others according to some random, shifting, arbitrary standard of attractiveness. We wrote letters to our bodies: how I am feeling *right now* about my body.

I wrote the following:

> Dear Body:
>
>   I feel energetic. Thanks.
>
>   The pain and fear of the last weeks have been awful. I think being ill or not in entirely good health has made my weight/ size issues of lesser importance.
>
>   If my gut stops hurting, I am grateful, not critical of it for sticking out.
>
>   Some outfits make me less ill at ease about my size or shape. Like tonight.
>
>   Although, tonight the thought of having supper with old college friends made me wonder if I've seen them since I got larger. I was glad to decline, this class to come to. The old stuff dies hard.
>
>   I am hoping you, my body, will be comfortable soon, that adjusting to the gall bladder removal runs its course and I can stop being fearful of a decline toward death.
>
>   Thanks, strong friend, for being mine. Love, Ruth

Volunteers read their letters aloud to the class, our attention to one another tender and respectful.

We finished that second evening together by assessing our present behavior, using a rating sheet designed by Susan Kano in her book, *Making Peace with Food* (Harper & Row, 1989). The assessment was designed for use "by anyone who wants to support health and well-being instead of diet/weight conflict and eating disorders."

In the first section, I recognized that I tease people about their eating habits, criticize (not as much as I used to) my own eating habits, and make negative comments about my fatness (no more, I wish!). The behaviors listed in the first section are what we call normal cultural responses, such as "assume someone is doing well because she has lost weight"; "presume that fat people want to lose weight"; refer to "good" and "bad" food; and talk about "being good" and "being bad" in reference to eating behavior.

The second section describes positive behaviors toward others, such as "encourage/approve of spontaneous eating, encourage someone to let go of guilt, openly admire a fat person's appearance, actively oppose fattism, challenge myths about diet and weight, discourage self-criticism and competitiveness, compliment someone's creativity, ideas, openness, efforts, sensitivity." The five-scale rating system allowed us to answer accurately and honestly. Something we think we do not *ever do*, if we're honest, might rate a "rarely"; conversely, something we think we're good about doing, might rank a "frequently" or "occasionally," not a "daily."

The last, more ambivalent-answer section, focuses on "talk about your appearance," "talk about someone else's appearance," "admire slenderness," "talk about your weight," "talk about calories." In all categories, and especially in this last section, over the years of using Kano's work, I have learned a lot of new behaviors, let go of old ones, and am generally sensitized to those comments and behaviors that support looksism and fattism, and those that help destroy the rationale for keeping women in a prison of their size and weight.

After thoughtfully going over these behavior categories, we select the specific areas we want to work on changing during the next week, write them out, tell a partner, and sign each other's contracts. We are also to be alert for fattist comments in the next week, or any remarks that support the "one size fits all/one must be one size" insanity for women.

There was a rhythm to our times together, one of ups and downs, hearing each other's stories, remembering our own histories, facing up to the vicious cultural barrage against large women, finding places in our worlds where we are affirmed, and where we affirm ourselves and each other. Ups and downs also defined the rhythm of our time apart, when we read the handout articles and the books that support our efforts, watched television, reviewed special videos, shopped, ate, went to work, exercised, and interacted with our families and others.

All of these extraordinarily complex circumstances were interwoven within and among the complexities of each of us, all winding, twining upward, into this new work of giving up what our world tells us about who we are and finding a new way to honor our bodies, our selves.

Chapter 24

Fighting Back

Kim lightened our spirits at the beginning of that third week with her story.

As she joined a volleyball game the past week, she heard murmured comments such as, "You're too fat to play," "You're no good at this," and "You can't play with us." Her answer to those rude, cruel, thoughtless comments was to play like an Amazon, ferociously, showing them the exact opposite of their long-held stereotypes. She was good at volleyball and let the dissenters—all male—know that a large woman can be in good shape, can exercise, and can be a good athlete.

Her fighting back led us to talk about what positive reactions we might devise and rehearse for the inevitable dreadful things people say to us. We all don't play volleyball nor are socialized to be assertive, but we figured we needed to work on speaking honestly and directly to people who think we are fair game for their prejudices.

Each week we reviewed and reviewed, and shared current evidences of the epidemic of fat hating and bashing from newspapers, magazines, TV watching, and things people say. We checked in regarding our homework. The small assignment of looking at one's self naked in a full-length mirror was difficult for most, impossible for some.

Despite the sexual revolution, as it is called, and the surfeit of sexually explicit material, including what is labeled pornography and/or exotic and what is permissible mainstream, we are still a Puritan culture, tsk-tsking at any improper nudity. Maybe I project, having grown up in my mother's Christian Science household in which neither bodily functions were mentioned nor was one's body honored by word or gesture, except that of remarking on weight and degrees of attractive or not. So well socialized to ignore my body and certainly never to show much of it, except in socially approved ways such as a bathing suit, I know how hard it is, even in the privacy of one's home, to be naked, to take a few minutes to look at my naked body in a mirror.

A most rewarding exercise was then to name one place where we felt good about ourselves. We had to rephrase this memory scan, since several women remembered feeling good about themselves when they were thin or a certain size or shape. We asked this question: Regardless of my weight or size, when was a time and place I felt good about myself?

Forever I remember that delicious night in a European spa in Denver, women's night, when I reveled in the naked bodies of at least 40 women of all sizes, shapes, ages, colors, wandering in and out of the whirlpool, the sauna, the showers, the steam room.

I remember canoeing the Niobrara River in northeast Nebraska and realizing we'd spent three days without mirrors, never being able to judge what we looked like, only able to see our plain, outdoor selves in each other—in bathing suits, cut-offs, T-shirts, canvas hats, sun cream, and smiles.

In class, we became a drama octet and read aloud to each other sections from *Parade* magazine's opinion letter page; in this case, teenagers writing in about how it feels to be skinny and how it feels to be fat.

A body-message review let us reflect and write the messages we receive about how our bodies looks, their physical abilities, their strengths/weaknesses, our bodies and their sexuality. We quickly wrote adjectives describing each part of our bodies that were listed on a sheet.

This memory scan and self-inventory simply give us more information about how we see ourselves, how we remember our family seeing us, and how much of a job it is to design a positive image of ourselves.

A simple tool for revealing to ourselves our positive qualities is headed "I am." We circled any of the 94 adjectives that we thought apply to ourselves, from "accepting" to "warm," "enterprising to "persuasive." I am forever amazed how many good words I am honestly able to apply to myself. One woman and I discovered no words on the sheet for sexual or sensuous so we added several adjectives to describe ourselves as sexual beings.

Across that sheet of paper, I find these scrawls to myself: "Oh, I wish this were easier. Sure we can sit here and talk, safe from the male gaze and the establishment world. Yet I give them, it, way too much power. Do I get to be an angry old woman? Do I never get to have someone take pleasure in my body? Can I do that? I am wary of this self-obsession and want to substitute Linda's word, reflection, for obsession."

A quick read through Susan Kano's faulty assumptions about weight, written in *Making Peace with Food*, helped us unlearn old untruths and learn their opposites. These faulty assumptions, with supporting information and documentation, are: fat people eat more than thin people; a slow metabolism is just an excuse; each person needs a certain number of calories to maintain her weight; being fat is unhealthy; fatness is caused by lifestyle, not heredity; and anyone can become and remain thin through a sensible diet. Such faulty assumptions are hazardous to our health and happiness and we need to learn the truth about them.

Finally, in our third class, we began to learn about our body's "setpoint." "Setpoint theory," in Kano's words, "explains the body's resistance to weight alteration . . . Examples of the body's attempts to defend its setpoint weight, the weight that is physiologically optimal, [are that] low-calorie diets cause metabolic decreases, while overfeeding causes metabolic increases" (pp. 19-25).

"Some of us are meant to be very thin; some of us are meant to be very fat; and most of us are meant to be somewhere in between," Kano explains, using the setpoint theory to explain the body's resistance to weight alteration, which she describes as "better than any other theory to date." She continues, "Setpoint weights are the result of both genetic influence *and* diet/lifestyle . . . Although lifestyle affects weight, we *inherit* our setpoint weight ranges."

Kano's sums up of this thoughtful, well-researched chapter with the following:

> We now know that you have a setpoint weight that your body is attempting to defend with strong physiological mechanism. If you try to override your setpoint through weight-loss diets,

an unhealthy and painful battle between your body and yourself is inevitable. Your body will adjust to lower caloric intake
through lower metabolic rates. And once you fall below your
setpoint, you may experience insatiability, food preoccupation,
strong cravings, extended taste responsiveness, decreased energy
levels, apathy, decreased sexual urges and responsiveness, ame-
norrhea (lack of periods), increased sensitivity to cold, general
irritability, and inexplicable depression.

Most of us believe that if we are unable to control our diet
and weight, it is due to personal weaknesses and psychological
problems. We repeatedly try to override and control our hunger in
order to attain and maintain lower weights. Our bodies try to
force us to give ourselves what we want and need (more food!);
and we try to force our bodies to "make do," continue to
function, and give up our body fat. We wage a war with our
own bodies.

The next week we began class by saying, "I am a beautiful,
powerful woman, and today I am proud of myself because . . . "
Most people do this verbal exercise by *leaving off the sentence
starter*, as if it is bragging or too odd to say such a thing. Another
opener is "Tonight I am feeling _____ about my weight and
appearance. Where I once felt better was _____."

We did two rounds, on separate nights, of bringing a *recent*
photograph of ourselves. The request was to bring a snapshot, not a
posed or studio photograph. Not so strangely, several women brought
their wedding photographs or a family photograph in which they had
just lost weight and looked slim, in addition to a recent snapshot.

Each woman would describe herself in the photograph, usually
with much negative comment; then we passed the photograph around
and each took a turn describing the woman we saw. We saw purpose, determination, joy *and* confusion, and sadness in each other's
faces and beautifully clothed bodies. We did not see fat or thin,
square or short, or pear-shaped in each other's photographs.

I discovered an amazing thing in one photo session. The women
in class described me in a snapshot as having a good time with a
friend, radiating fun and joy. Surprised at their reactions, I looked
again at the snapshot of myself. Instead of bringing the photograph

taken by someone who is decidedly uncomfortable with my size and clothing, which I thought I had, I had accidentally picked up one taken on the same occasion by someone else who sent it to me. That second person obviously thought it was a good enough picture to send to me, and obviously liked it and how I looked that day, since she sent me the photo. Although taken on the same occasion, the two photographs, taken by two different people, showed the same woman, looking different.

A startling fact is that I *do* see myself through another's eyes— that particular vision recorded in a photograph, another's vision of what I look like! I would not have thought this possible unless I saw it happen with my own eyes, these two separate visions recorded in two photographs of me taken at almost the same moment.

Our first photograph session led to a discussion of clothing: Who dressed us as a child? How do we shop today? How do we dress ourselves for a day alone at home or a day out in the world? With whose eyes do we dress ourselves as we think of the people we will see that day? Who do we see when we look in the mirror?

A serendipitous moment in class led us to list all the things our bodies do. My list included walk, swim, bike, sit, eat, sleep, stretch, wiggle, lift, carry, hurry, rest, hug, touch, pat, shiver, shake, write, draw, type, move about, do yoga sun salutes, in a later class I made a list of 5 things I didn't think of in that moment. The idea is to recognize what a valuable functioning organism is this body we live in.

One of the homework assignments was to focus on a positive attribute of ourselves every time we looked in a mirror or saw our reflection in a store window that week. As well, we were to beware of "head shots" only, which falls into the "She has such a pretty face" syndrome of one insulting way the world views large/fat/ heavy women.

Strategies we used more than once, some several times, were the photograph session; the 24-hour body-clothing inventory; the technique of stating "Regardless of my weight, I felt good about my body when . . . ; additions to our diet history; sharing of that week's collection of media images of women and/or comments we had to endure; letters to ourselves regarding 'Right now I am feeling about my body . . . '"; and discussions of our homework reading for that week.

More often than not the scheduled class exercises and strategies would lead to unexpected discussions, would point out directions we needed to explore right then, and would often lead to serendipitous moments.

Night after night, I would drive home, amazed at how our time together brought us into community; shored up our solidarity with one another; produced extraordinary vulnerability, tenderness, and hilarity; and exposed those things we desperately needed to talk about and never before found the safe place to do that. Yet, that two hours one night a week for six weeks was never long enough for us to tell our stories enough to be healed. Although the class was a giant step along the way to renewed strength, self-empowerment and self-acceptance, it was only part of the journey.

Our need for companions on this journey cannot be met by an occasional class. We must find ways to meet, to connect regularly, to walk together out of the prison of appearance and toward that new land where who we are is just perfect.

Chapter 25

Images of Ourselves–Good and Awful

An awful silence hung in our classroom. We had just watched Jean Kilbourne's new video *Slim Hopes—Advertising and the Obsession with Thinness*. An older woman spoke first: "That depresses me. I feel so terrible." Others agreed with her feelings and expressed other reactions, such as anger, fury, disbelief, and of being overwhelmed.

This compelling, powerful, 30-minute video gives us a hard look at the reality we live in today. Watching Jean Kilbourne's videos, including the equally devastating portraits culled from magazines, store windows, and newspapers in *Killing Us Softly*, and *Still Killing Us Softly*, as well as *Calling the Shots*—all of which are concerned with what advertising does to American women—cracks wide open our denial of reality.

Slim Hopes opens with Annie Lennox singing "Keep Young and Beautiful, If you want to be loved" as a satiric background. Kilbourne narrates slides of current advertisements, insisting that advertising isn't the only purveyor of stereotypes in our lives, but certainly the most persuasive and pervasive with which we are surrounded.

The advertisements, from magazines and newspapers, are deconstructed to show these realities: dismemberment of women's bodies; women's bodies as possessions; the "little girl" look to disempower grown women; encouragement of binge eating; shame around our bodies and food; impossible flawlessness pictured by combining body parts of several women and computer imaging; the exaggerated fit look; glaring conflicts typical of advertising to women illustrated by a *Women's Day* cover heralding "85 ways to lose weight" and "a ten-minute ice cream pie"; using food for emotional needs (usually loss of a man), at least control over our bodies (implicit: we have no other power); eating described in religious terms (sinful, salvation, forgiveness, bad); women's appetites for food disparaged, an obvious double standard between men and women; food as the enemy; food advertised as a substitute for sex; women's bodies as the actual product; women's bodies referred to in food terms (peaches, honey, tomato); and smoking targeted at women and young girls clearly implying that smoking keeps you thin (the adjectives slim, slender, sleek used to describe cigarettes).

Kilbourne, after years of research and study in how advertising uses and affects American women, finds all these advertising distortions "deliberate," reminding us that their primary purpose is to sell products, as the primary purpose of the publication is to sell its pages to advertisers.

I was delighted and appalled at the not-so-subliminal message in cigarette advertisements I saw recently. One featured a romantic-looking man and woman. In another, one woman is smoking, and the words printed below her say, "Who says length doesn't matter?" Sure, they are talking about the length of the cigarette, not a particular penis.

An especially illuminating page in *Ms.* magazine, which does not carry advertising, finding that inimical to its purpose of honesty and strength for women, is the "No Comment" section at the back, where images of women in advertisements are reprinted, often horrifying in their violence and sadism.

Barraging her listeners with relentless statistics, *Slim Hopes*'s Kilbourne reports that 11.3 percent of young women are bulimic, 10 percent of college women are anorexic, and nine out of ten young women can be considered obsessed with food and worried about their weight. Kilbourne also provides us with these startling facts:

"80 percent of fourth grade girls are on diets."

"Twenty years ago, models body weight was 8 percent below the average, now it is 23 percent below. Models represent the body type of 5 percent of American women."

"Most [models] have had breast implants . . . since this body type (tall, genetically thin, broad-shouldered, narrow hips) generally has small breasts."

Pitching diets to girls "leads to osteoporosis . . . is harmful . . . and takes years to undo the damage."

"The diet industry, which did not exist 20 years ago, is a $33 *billion* industry."

"50 percent of American women are dieting at any one time."

"Three-fourths of normal-weight women think they are over-weight."

"98 percent of all dieters lose back the lost weight and gain more."

"More young girls are smoking than ever before. The tobacco industry needs 3,000 children to start smoking every day to replace those who die or quit. 90 percent of smokers start before they are 18, and 60 percent start before high school."

In a survey of American adult women, given one thing they wanted to change, more than half responded by wanting to lose weight. Given three magic wishes, girls between 11 and 17, by an overwhelming margin, listed losing and keeping off weight at number one.

In a world that is "increasingly violent and unpredictable, with the increasing likelihood of environmental destruction, in which we are increasingly powerless," Kilbourne reasons, "at least [we are told] we can keep our bodies in control."

Underlying these messages is "the fear of women . . . so women are supposed to be fragile, small, keep their voices high . . . have a little girl look."

"Thinness is today's equivalent of virginity. If food is sex, the good girl is the one who keeps all her appetites under control. The fat girl or woman is the bad girl." The food advertising budget in this country is currently at $36 billion. (I find this statistic fascinating. We do have to eat to live, and the majority in the United States have enough or more than enough to eat; yet we may be encouraged to be obsessed with food by its $36 billion dollar *advertising* budget, light years away from subsistence farming and gardening.)

"One of the last socially acceptable forms of prejudice" is making negative, critical comments [even] in front of large or considered to be large women, Kilbourne continues.

Citing the *Ladies Home Journal* as one of the women's magazines "that make women obsess about their weight," Kilbourne reiterates the empowering and important truth that "it is profitable for advertisers for women to feel terrible about themselves."

"This is not a trivial issue," she insists. "It cuts to the heart of women's energy, power, and self-esteem. It is a major public health problem that endangers women's lives. Individual treatment will not solve it. We must change the environment, change the norms of dieting and thinness."

"The truth is that women come in all sizes and shapes," Kilbourne asserts. She recommends freeing our imaginations from the images with which we are surfeited through entering into dialogue with others about this issue; through women supporting women, joining the anti-diet movement, and working toward wellness: by feeling good about ourselves and not allowing "others to rob us of the real avenue to power and self-esteem in this attempt to limit women's power."

"We must become media literate, critical viewers, work to eliminate gender bias, and help women and girls develop authentic roots to power, to break free of the narrow images that imprison us," Kilbourne asserts.

I have long loved Jean Kilbourne's fine work, the intelligence and courage she brings to deconstruction of the media's influence on women, through her personal writings, research, and appearances, and through the Media Education Foundation (26 Center St., Northampton, MA 01060).

One piece of our work that springs from the life-changing pain of facing the truth of advertising images is to make a list of "things I do to feel better about myself." Our wild and wonderful lists included massages, daily exercise, sleep, attendance at 12-step groups, eating, writing, movies, quiet time, being alone, baths, trips, reading, and letting go of whatever anger we can release.

With all the brilliant solutions to life's difficulties available, I am finding again those small places in my life that liberate my spirit. I recognize as soul-feeding that half hour a day, at my favorite coffee shop, or alone in my kitchen, drinking tea and reading from my backlog of progressive magazines. Another is walking out of my swimming pool at sunset, clean and refreshed, endorphins released in my blood.

Listening in the quiet of an early Saturday evening to an especially sorrowful and tender "Life in Lake Woebegon" with Garrison Keillor gathers my world into a tiny whole. My favorite remains the poignant "The Day the Babe Ruth All-Stars Came to Lake Woebegon."

Something serendipitous will make me feel better about myself.

Getting work done, although verging on my obsessive workaholism, releases energy and makes me less picky about life. Brenda Ueland, a splendid woman who died at 93 after a rich and vital life, speaks directly to my writing heart, especially when she says, "Why should we all use our creative power . . .? Because there is nothing that makes people so generous, joyful, lively, bold and compassionate, so indifferent to fighting and the accumulation of objects and money" (*If You Want to Write*, Graywolf Press, 1987). I *always* feel like a grown-up, able to go about in the world more easily after some hours of writing.

Petting my cat ranks right up there with slowing down, me and Booger-Barrabas both purring. I look forward to one of my favorite NBA teams on television at night, or a British mystery program (Inspector Morse or detective Jane Tennison), or a new Sara Paretsky or Sue Grafton mystery book. Eating crackers and milk at midnight; hearing a Saul Landau commentary on Pacifica Radio as I drive downtown to teach a class or home from the swimming pool, or Bailey White reporting from her life in south Georgia on NPR bring me delight.

In the class, we also journaled about "My body does/is." I wrote that my body is strong and extremely functional, exercises, is responsive to touch, learns well, drives a car, walks downstairs, walks upstairs, resists carrying heavy loads, loves being in my favorite white cotton nightgown, touches others, breathes, sleeps well and long, likes snuggling in bed with my husband, eats healthy good food, responds to reduced stress, feels good right this minute, and wears earrings. All that fine stuff found in five minutes!

We felt stronger with the information from *Slim Hopes*, knowing that pretending not to know what we know robs us of the will to action in our lives.

From the Filmakers Library in New York City, I received to preview three videos that had been shown at the *Enduring Spirit, Women As We Age* conference. Produced by the University of

Nebraska at Omaha's College of Continuing Studies, it is a conference full of energy and wisdom for hundreds of women, at which I
have presented for several years.

She's Not Fat, She's My Mom left me with conflicted feelings. A
young man produced this documentary of his mother's "compulsive
overeating," in which during the 20-weeks filming time she lost 40
pounds and began to feel better about herself, still a large woman.
Although the filming was of people whose attitudes reflect their
reality, I was disturbed by the assumption that weighing more than
average meant there was something wrong with John Spellos'
mother, and by the obvious anger at and disinterest in his wife's
welfare, evidenced by the husband. I got chills to hear the mother/
wife/woman say "All our lives, people have controlled us and the
only thing we can control is what we eat." A skilled mental health
counselor and a woman not entirely cowed by life, despite her size
and weight, Amy found ways "to be myself" despite years of abuse
from her parents and her husband. She tells us, "What we must learn
to do is love ourselves . . . and through therapy deal with all forms of
abuse."

I found *Beautiful Piggies*, produced by Barbara Bader, to be
extraordinarily painful—a document of a women's weight and eating problems as photographed by Bader and narrated by the woman,
her husband, and parents. Called "vastly overweight" by her husband, who adds, "I don't think she's even been trying [to lose
weight]," he states flatly, "The reason she is overweight is because
she's eating too much food and . . . I'd like to know the underlying
reasons." This video's assumption is that weight over average is due
to overeating and bingeing, and that the weight is a problem for the
woman only, not her large father who remembers, "we were always
concerned about her weight, she was chubby then, not obese like
now. After all she had to catch a guy someday." The young woman
"star" of *Beautiful Piggies* agrees she has a "weight problem" and
talks a lot about "fairly long periods of depression" as a child,
describing her food obsessions and remembering "When I was thin
I felt I was in control of myself." Ending with quotes from Susie
Orbach's *Fat Is a Feminist Issue*, *Beautiful Piggies* joins the war
against fat, which considers more than average weight pathological,

an indication of deep psychological problems, and that something is wrong with the person.

The Old Bags' Club, produced by George James for the Canadian Broadcasting Company, is a fierce real-life discussion among women who have been dumped by long-term husbands for younger—and thinner—women. The story begins with Sally Moon, a woman who lives in southwest England, who erupted in rage at her husband's treatment of her. After cutting up all his fancy suits, pouring 12 liters of white paint over his car, and smashing his wine collection in the middle of the village, she gained media attention and correspondence with other women in similar circumstances. Sally came to realize, "[It] isn't the end of the world . . . but I wish he'd been honest with me [instead of having an affair]. There are so many of us, we're just wall paper. I've seen survival . . . and I knew I could. I was determined not to give in no matter how tough it is." The women interviewed for *The Old Bags' Club* all felt "cheated of our futures without our husbands. . . . Suddenly to find yourself alone, and feel old . . . changing horses mid-stream, only women can help. . . . For 30 years [he told me] I was fat, dumb and stupid . . . and left me to grow old alone while seeking rejuvenation with a younger woman." These women found that "men our age (50's) are looking for young women. Why pick up an empty bag, which is what we are?" At this point, they began to learn how to survive, to find each other, to rebuild their sense of themselves as valuable, interesting women, and to make a life without needing the approval or affirmation of men. (All three films are available from Filmakers Library, 124 E. 40th Street, New York, NY, 10016.)

We also viewed, from my own video collection, Katherine Gilday's *The Famine Within* (Direct Cinema Limited), a documentary of "the contemporary obsession with body size and shape among North American women," which, although honest and provocative, does not substantially address the issues of institutional oppression; *Throwing Our Weight Around* from Roundabout Productions, produced by Sandy Dwyer, is a rolicking, somber, courageous documentary about large women daring to feel good about themselves; and the FAT LIP Reader's Theatre's *Nothing to Lose* offers several skits by this radical San Francisco performance troup. Some of the women in class could not identify with the very large women portrayed in the last two videos. An honest, provocative film about women growing old, *Acting Our Age* is excellent (also from Direct Cinema Limited, P.O. Box 69799, Los Angeles, CA 90069).

Although we waded through reams of information and literature in our six weeks together, we also understood that many of the liberating solutions are to be found within ourselves and are waiting to be called forth as ready and willing companions full of strength and courage for this journey.

Chapter 26

Steps to Freedom

As we came together for our final class, I reminded the courageous women voyagers that the point of all our reading, talking, writing, researching, reflecting, is

- to learn to love our bodies,
- to learn to eat spontaneously,
- to learn to love ourselves,
- to learn to sort out our values,
- to express our rights and needs,
- to develop healthy lifestyles,
- to get support from each other, and
- to find the energy to take our own steps to freedom.

We read through and answered Susan Kano's "Person Questions: Transforming Your Body Image" (p. 61) in *Making Peace with Food*. Practically a PhD thesis, the 26 telling, thorough questions included "What did you think about your body before you began to worry about diet and weight?"; "How often do you weigh yourself?"; "Do you hide yourself in very baggy or unexciting clothing"; "How do you judge other people on the basis of their appearance?"; "Think of at least three specific things you can do to try to counteract societal influences that support diet/weight preoccupation"; and "Imagine that you are completely at peace with your body and yourself . . . Describe what you think and feel about yourself and your body, as if it were true."

Kano precedes this questionnaire with "Important Goals to Keep in Mind." It is a list we all could keep posted on the fridge, or on our bathroom mirror:

1. See your body as a trusted and treasured home for yourself to enjoy and use fully, rather than as an aesthetic object.
2. Enrich and broaden your aesthetically thin mind: notice beauty in everyone around you.
3. Replace fattism with respect for all people regardless of size.
4. See people as whole human beings, rather than objects with certain physical characteristics.
5. Stop weighing yourself. Get rid of your scale if you have one.
6. Stop using your weight and weight control as a measure of your value; value yourself simply for who you are.
7. Clothe yourself comfortably and pleasingly, knowing that you deserve to be comfortable.
8. Increase your physical pleasure and decrease your physical discomfort as much as possible.
9. Reject the destructive social prescription to be as thin as possible in your every thought, word, and action.

A personal action plan (I saved from some workshop, somewhere!) asked that we write down some ways to begin appreciating our bodies. I changed the plan's "pamper" your body to "nurture" your body. "Pamper" sounds like babying one's self, instead of taking self-respecting and nurturing action. On old copies of this sheet, I have written vows to go to the hot tubs at least once a week, to be naked in front of a mirror with intention, and to bring pleasure to myself in other ways—all of which I forget to do, do not want to do so, do not think of them, and, that oldest of excuses, figure I am too busy to do.

In order to practice "loving and accepting my body unconditionally," this exercise includes an affirmation of acceptance and commitment and a suggested visualization.

Marcia Germaine Hutchinson's fine book *Transforming Body Image, Learning to Love the Body You Have* (The Crossing Press, 1985) is full of imagery and visualizations that might constitute the agenda for several (10 to 20) weeks work together for a group of women. I can imagine how one's image of one's self would be remarkably better after such an experience.

However, Hutchinson is of that group of experts who still use the word "overweight" as if it were an agreed-upon measure; and she also recommends such things as "there is room for improvement when I'm ready" and that negative feelings about our bodies lead some to "turn down invitations, stay home and eat and feel sorry for ourselves," as if staying separate from a social scene and being at home means eating more than our bodies want or is disturbing anti-social behavior. As well, she asserts that "a good healthy, positive body image is essential before we can learn *how to eat and bring our weight within the proper range and keep it there* [emphasis mine]," and "if we decide that a diet is necessary, our chances of succeeding and keeping the weight off are immeasurably improved if we diet lovingly."

I find some of such beliefs illustrative of the fox in the chicken coop, so to speak, assuming that all women want to lose weight, and defining as sacrosanct women's desire to lose weight, diet, or find some external measurement of their size and weight. I suspect Weight Watchers and the Diet Center and all the others recommend dieting "lovingly."

We made notes to ourselves about what was the most meaningful work we did, which was, unanimously, the sharing and honesty, what changes we could make in our lives (from the personal action plan list; mine included "move as if I were gorgeous") the "assessing present behavior" chart we did in second week, and other choices and decisions we made; and where we could get support for our efforts. We looked at those places where we can stop expecting support, by what timelines would we proceed with our work, and what we are aware of that stops us. I noted that my own unconscious resistance to change could interfere with loving my body, as does focusing on what someone else thinks or tells me, trying to gain acceptance from "the establishment," competitiveness and comparing myself with other women, and not taking enough time to let my awareness expand, to learn, reflect, and change.

Again turning to *Making Peace with Food* (p. 200), we remind ourselves of the frequently offered "solutions" to weight problems, ones we might be holding in the back of our minds as *THE* way to feel better about ourselves:

> Temporary weight-loss diets "promote diet/weight preoccupation and eating disorders without providing any lasting positive effects.

The only option more harmful than a weight-loss diet is probably a weight-loss diet with "diet pills."

Programmed eating allows no spontaneous eating and "simulates the release from eating decisions . . . [although it] has provided many people with desperately needed relief . . . and can be used as a temporary measure . . . although a sorry replacement for freedom.

Overeaters Anonymous continues to promote the idea that the sufferer is powerless and that compulsive overeating and related disorders are incurable—that one's Higher Power can control the symptoms but one can never be completely free of the "illness." This is simply untrue.

Permanent change of diet [would require] us to shop differently, cook differently, and avoid a large proportion of the foods we are offered by other people. . . difficult to maintain. . . The key is to be patient and avoid focusing on weight loss as the goal or reason behind your dietary changes . . . make the changes slowly but surely . . . enjoy eating, avoid being fanatical or rigid about the choices you make, eat in harmony with your hunger and satiation, and try to keep dieters' mind-set from creeping into your efforts.

Exercise programs are among the best of the pseudosolutions. Unfortunately, many exercise programs focus on people's desire to "improve" their appearance through weight loss.

We reviewed ways to expand appreciation of our bodies, to love people of all sizes, to undermine objectification, to develop an instrumental body view, relearn spontaneous eating, develop life-supportive values, and learn to love ourselves and gain cooperation from family and friends.

Our finale was to brainstorm the ways and means we could effect in our daily lives to break free!

Writing as fast as I could, I took down the women's suggestions: yoga, stretch, swim, wear bathing suits/bikinis, dance, belly-dance, stair-walk, wear funky clothes, get hair done, get a makeover, have a massage, indulge, take this class, keep going, eat what you want when you want it, go out in public, go with and feel as good as our thin friends, eat in front of people, start a support group, share, dress complimentarily, flirt, go to husband's business social affairs, water-ski, subscribe to *Radiance* ($20 a year, P.O. Box 30246, Oakland, CA 94604), request large women catalogs, fight back against convention, watch good videos, stand up to rude comments, talk about media issues, recommend Jean Kilbourne videos, join NAFTA (National Association for Fat Acceptance, P.O. Box 188620, Sacramento, CA 95818), write to companies about offensive commercials, object to being asked our weight, stop weighing, accept compliments, be naked in front of a mirror, repeat the photograph sessions, have a fashion show for large women, speak no put-downs of others, deflect criticism by turning a deaf ear, counter health versus weight attitude, stop dieting, stop talking about diets, weight, and food, quit wishing "If only I were thin," quit scapegoating our bodies to avoid other issues, work on posture, move as if we find ourselves beautiful, do imagery and meditations, think, write, get rid of old clothes, throw out or move scales, do not read women's magazines regarding diets, subscribe to *MS.*, check out the opposition, petition clothing stores not to separate large women's clothing into special sections (frankly, I like to have the clothes for large women in a defined area so I can enjoy the company of other women my size and not sort through a rack beside someone who wears acceptable sizes), compliment integration, tuck in blouses, wear short skirts, don't try to hide size, get some style advice, get "colors" done, don't laugh with others who laugh at fat jokes or cartoons, always respond to offensive material with a letter or a boycott, tell friends, use your size positively, nurture ourselves, have time outdoors, clean out closets, find reasons to laugh, hot tub, be visible, express all emotions, be sexual, be sensuous, turn off TV, indulge, sweat, lift weights, wear silky things, take long baths, use lotion on body, get comfortable being naked, exercise for endorphin rush, wear bright colors, let a breeze flow over naked body, do the work even if it's painful, volunteer to give presentations on weight and size, rock the boat, enter model searches for large women, ask that fashion shows include all sizes, know it is good and okay to take care of ourselves, continue writing 24-hour body/food inventories and diet histories, and read all the books we reviewed and reflected on in class. (At a recent workshop, the women added *not* subscribing to any women's magazines, except *Ms.*, and touching ourselves lovingly, overcoming that taboo against self-touch.)

What the women said that last night was that being together and talking to and listening to each other was the thing that helped us the most. We certainly could have met for a longer time, and for several more weeks, but we had made a start; we began the long journey out of the women's prison of defining ourselves by our appearances, and toward that scary freedom of being totally, only, and beautifully ourselves.

After the classes were over, I discovered that I felt better about myself, was less concerned with what other people thought, less sensitive to what I thought others might be thinking, able to get dressed and go about in my world more comfortably, and generally stronger and happier.

These feelings did not disappear after a while, as peak experiences are apt to do. Working on this book has increased my feelings of both comfort and discomfort with weight and appearance issues. However, I still have a long way to go to be free of any discomfort about my appearance, to totally accept myself as fit and attractive, as beautiful. My "beautiful" horizons have broadened enormously in regard to other women; now I need to include myself in that rich, vibrant consciousness.

Most days, I am glad to be on this hard and unexpected journey into a bewildering and exciting new land, simply one requirement of entrance to a vital old age.

Epilogue

100-Plus Ways to Fight Ageism, Looksism, Sexism, Racism, Fatism

Say hello to every old or large woman you see. Especially greet with cheer fat, skinny, or differently-abled old women.

Don't buy birthday cards that make fun of aging. They nearly all do.

Tell people how old you are.

Call yourself old if you are over 60, counting life in thirds.

Don't pretend people can't tell which is the mother and which is the daughter.

Don't greet people with how young (or thin!) they look.

Never say, "You're just as young as you feel," or "Old is just a state of mind." Both mean young is good, old is bad.

Do not say to yourself, "At my age . . ." Such a phrase always disparages.

Consider giving up wearing makeup.

Consider not dyeing your hair.

Regarding makeup and hair dye, consider the path your sister must walk.

Do not describe another woman by saying, "She has such a pretty face."

Choose to wear clothes that feel comfortable, not ones that are especially fashionable.

Think about your shoes: what is good for your back, your feet, your comfort?

Do not be talked into buying something because "it makes you look thin" or "hides your tummy."

Figure out some guerilla action against the euphemisms for and acts of torture we call cosmetic surgery, that is, the cutting and rearranging of our bodies in order to be "more attractive."

Think about the real meaning of "face *lift*," "*tummy tuck*," "*lipo-*suction," "nose *job*," "eye *tuck*," "breast *enhancement*," "*cosmetic surgery*," and "chin *lift*."

Always refer to optional "cosmetic surgery" as *cutting up* our (usually women's) bodies.

Give up dieting.

Eat what your body needs and what you want.

Think how much space you (are permitted to) take up in the world.

Be angry, even inappropriately.

Talk too loud.

Refuse to be a wise old woman.

Honor your own wisdom.

Do not cast your pearls before swine.

Find a place to hang out with young people, practice treating yourself as an equal in their presence.

Do not live in age-segregated housing projects, unless you have to.

Look around your house, the places you go: Can a person using a walker get around there? Use the bathroom? Can a heavy person walk without stress from point A to point B? Are there railings to hold onto? Are the seats wide enough for large people?

Consider this: can every ailment you experience be chalked up to old age?

Demand that doctors who tell you, "You're not getting any younger, you know" explain what they mean.

Refuse to be weighed at your medical office, unless it is directly related to the condition for which you are there. Ask the connection between your condition and what you weigh, or how old you are.

Do not use "old" as a bad word. Use it often, to describe an age, not one's attitude.

Talk to large and/or old women at all social gatherings.

Resist thinking that only extroverts and socially adept people are worthy.

Read Cynthia Rich, Barbara McDonald, Naomi Wolf (*Beauty Myth* only), Becky Thompson, Susan Faludi, Carolyn Heilbrun, Ruth Harriet Jacobs, Helen Luke, Nelle Morton, May Sarton, Florida Scott-Maxwell, Barbara Walker, Meridel Le Sueur, and Shevy Healey.

Look at Elizabeth Layton's drawings and paintings.

Even though it publishes no longer, do not think of *Lear's* magazine as good for old women. It was for rich, white, thin, "successful" women.

Subscribe to *MS.*, which refuses to carry advertising, rightly considering that counter-productive to women's freedom.

Use your time wisely. Despite what most religions tell us, as far as we know, our life is finite, our years limited.

Look people in the eye.

Stop worrying about the children.

Stop parenting your grown children. (Barbara McDonald)

Pay attention to your life.

Refuse to await, as Carolyn Heilbrun puts it, another chapter in the heterosexual plot.

Know the freedom from fulfilling the needs of others and from being a female impersonator. (Heilbrun)

Do not allow yourself to be "captured by regret, resentment or despair." (Heilbrun)

Decide "whether to live as a different woman or die as a woman trying to be young." (Heilbrun)

Dump "the baggage of the male gaze" (Heilbrun)

Do not "brood on how one looks or disappoints." (Heilbrun)

If you cannot shut off your TV, strictly ration your time watching it.

Do not read women's magazines that propagandize getting and keeping a man, dieting, cooking, appearance, etc.

Write letters to editors, businesses, advertisers, anyone or any institution whose practices offend you as an aging or large woman.

Watch out for the self-hater (Starhawk); he or she is everywhere but especially lives inside you and tells you he or she is your friend.

Go naked.

Love your body, under *all* conditions.

Wear camouflage if you must.

Do not envy the power of youth.

Get more safe, therapeutic touch.

Do not listen to men so much. Let them practice hearing you.

Complain about head tables.

Refuse to enter competitions.

Only belong to organizations that single-slate their elections and those that practice consensus and self-selection for various jobs.

Barter.

Meditate.

Breathe deeply.

Understand that even old women deny age hatred.

Don't expect old women to mother or grandmother you.

Take turns speaking, speak from experience, don't interrupt, and don't deliver judgments upon one another. (Barbara Deming)

Clean up your past.

Practice forgiveness, especially of yourself, again and again and again and again [as Shelly Kopp tells us in his Eschatological Laundry List, a partial register of the 927 (or was it 928?) Eternal Truths].

Speak your own truth, not someone else's. You will have to think hard and long to separate yourself from other's expectations and desires.

Do not take care of your grandchildren unless it is clearly your path (which does not mean when there's no one else to do it).

Resist "aging gracefully."

Ask people what they mean by "aging gracefully."

Do something outrageous every day. (Maggie Kuhn)

Remember that "*out*rage" keeps our rage making a difference in the world, and not turned in on ourselves.

Claim and celebrate your sexual identity.

Say what you feel.

Laugh loudly.

Be willing to let people see you cry.

Practice not being embarrassed, no matter the situation.

Stop saying, "If only . . . "

Stop saying, "I'm sorry."

When people say "She or he hasn't changed a whit," ask yourself why they think it's a compliment.

If you have to tell someone they look wonderful, do not base it on size, weight, color, style, hair, clothing, skin, or whether or not they are smiling.

Do not consider everyone unlike you "other." The rules are written in the United States to favor men, people of Anglo-Saxon heritage, heterosexuals, people with money, and people and groups with power. That does not make them the standard to which "others" repair.

Resist those who tell you to "smile."

Be careful of people who insist "everything's going to turn out alright."

Understand that not everyone walks the same road.

Know that you must find and follow yours.

Get together often with like-minded people.

Be careful about making yourself a target. It will wear you out.

Speak up when others make fun of other people, especially women.

Resist male-defined standards of beauty for females.

Look long at the Willendorf Goddess figure.

Move out of that safe harbor of acceptability. (Barbara McDonald)

Do not use words such as "seniors, elders, golden agers," and other words that substitute for *old*. (Elders of a tribe is specific and honorable.)

Examine your addiction to convention, good-girl-ism, respectability, and conformity.

Design your own rituals and traditions.

Stay curious.

Attend to unfinished business.

Do not let others tell you not to be depressed or sad. Grief has its seasons. Honor them.

Beware of the new stereotype of the marathon-running grandmother. She is not the only role model.

Know the difference between aging and ageism.

Figure out how you want to live your remaining years.

Learn to live with loss and death. Prepare for your own death, even if it upsets those around you.

If you don't want to be invisible, make people notice you, in grocery lines, on the street, in stores, at rallies, in committee meetings. Demand that attention be paid.

Do not let people interrupt you.

Don't let the bastards get you down.

Wild or shy, you have a right to be here, to be treated like a worthwhile human being.

Be "luminous with age," as Meridel LeSueur writes in "Rites of Ancient Ripening."

Do not use "feisty" to describe an angry woman, or one who speaks up loudly.

Know the profound truth of Dorothy Sayers' words, that "time and trouble will tame an advanced young woman, but an advanced old woman is uncontrollable by any earthly force."

Break the silence.

Celebrate the sacrament of the present moment.

Understand that people fear old women (and large women) for their power, for their knowledge, for breaking the rules, for their experience of this last stage of life, for claiming their own selves.

Remember what Muriel Rukeyser prophesied: What would happen if one woman told the truth about her life? The world would split open.

One hundred and nineteen is just a beginning. Continue among ourselves. Write your own list.

Index

Order Your Own Copy of
This Important Book for Your Personal Library!

FAT—A FATE WORSE THAN DEATH?
Women, Weight, and Appearance

_____ in hardbound at $39.95 (ISBN: 0-7890-0178-0)

_____ in softbound at $19.95 (ISBN: 1-56023-908-5)

COST OF BOOKS _____

OUTSIDE USA/CANADA/
MEXICO: ADD 20% _____

POSTAGE & HANDLING _____
(US: $3.00 for first book & $1.25
for each additional book)
Outside US: $4.75 for first book
& $1.75 for each additional book)

SUBTOTAL _____

IN CANADA: ADD 7% GST _____

STATE TAX _____
(NY, OH & MN residents, please
add appropriate local sales tax)

FINAL TOTAL _____
(If paying in Canadian funds,
convert using the current
exchange rate. UNESCO
coupons welcome.)

☐ **BILL ME LATER:** ($5 service charge will be added)
(Bill-me option is good on US/Canada/Mexico orders only;
not good to jobbers, wholesalers, or subscription agencies.)

☐ Check here if billing address is different from
shipping address and attach purchase order and
billing address information.

Signature _____

☐ **PAYMENT ENCLOSED: $** _____

☐ **PLEASE CHARGE TO MY CREDIT CARD.**

☐ Visa   ☐ MasterCard   ☐ AmEx   ☐ Discover
☐ Diner's Club

Account # _____

Exp. Date _____

Signature _____

Prices in US dollars and subject to change without notice.

NAME _____

INSTITUTION _____

ADDRESS _____

CITY _____

STATE/ZIP _____

COUNTRY _____ COUNTY (NY residents only) _____

TEL _____ FAX _____

E-MAIL_____
May we use your e-mail address for confirmations and other types of information? ☐ Yes   ☐ No

Order From Your Local Bookstore or Directly From
The Haworth Press, Inc.
10 Alice Street, Binghamton, New York 13904-1580 • USA
TELEPHONE: 1-800-HAWORTH (1-800-429-6784) / Outside US/Canada: (607) 722-5857
FAX: 1-800-895-0582 / Outside US/Canada: (607) 772-6362
E-mail: getinfo@haworth.com
PLEASE PHOTOCOPY THIS FORM FOR YOUR PERSONAL USE.

BOF96

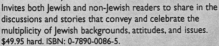
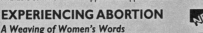
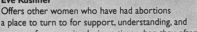